'As irreverent and incisive as the

HOW TO

LOVE

YOUR DONORS

(TO DEATH)

Stephen Pidgeon FInstF

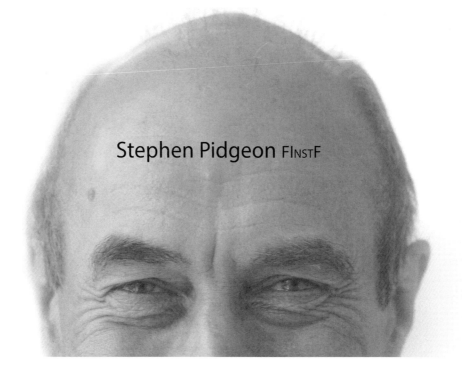

DIRECTORY OF SOCIAL CHANGE

HOW TO LOVE YOUR DONORS (to death!)

How to love your donors (to death)
Foreword, by **Ken Burnett**

I love this book with its clever title, practical content and overdue messages. And I'm delighted to see my long-time friend, colleague and respected competitor Stephen Pidgeon finally getting his take on donor relationship development into print. But I have to confess, I despair that it had to be written at all.

But written it had to be and Stephen has done us all a service in the process.

The striking thing about the case for exemplary donor care is that it's such evident moral and financial common sense. Yet common sense is not common at all and 'the bleedin' obvious' still manages to elude so many.

What is it about making donors feel good and treating them as if they're extra special that so many fundraisers, CEOs and trustee boards find so hard to grasp? Why, when good causes have nothing more to offer in return for freely-given financial support than the warm glow and good feeling of having done something really worth doing, do so many imagine that it isn't imperative that we ensure every donor enjoys the experience so much that they'll willingly give again and again because being a donor makes them feel, consistently, so good?

The evidence that most fundraisers don't get this enough to change it, is clear from the experiences of current and lapsed donors. It can be seen from donors who hang up or cross the street to avoid talking to a fundraiser. It's underlined by the repeated dismal results of countless 'mystery shopping' tests of charity responses to an unsolicited donation. And it's evident from the inexorable toll of that dread horseman of the fundraising apocalypse, Attrition, the super-expensive, energy-sapping, all-but-overwhelming nemesis of donor-focused fundraisers everywhere, the fundraising devil who keeps our causes small, weak and under-achieving by causing potential long-term donors to leave in droves.

Attrition of course is not the right name for this tragedy. More accurately we should call it what it is – today's professional fundraisers failing to keep their donors.

What prevents us from shaking off the dead hand of attrition is that as a sector we consistently fail to grasp the need for sustained major investment in the customer experience. When we see how completely the likes of Amazon have wrenched dominance of the book-buying market from the feeble grasp of a traditionalist, fragmented, under-investing book trade just by providing a painless, consistent, exemplary customer experience, we realise that fundraisers could never aspire to emulate such a thing. The so-called not-for-profit sector (which really should change its name to the for-change sector) is too lacking in vision and unity, too hamstrung by short-term thinking and stunted by under-investment and the twin daft notions of cost ratios and immediate return on investment to ever aspire to putting such a grand vision into practice.

A bright light these last three decades on the international fundraising stage, Stephen Pidgeon needs little introduction to seasoned fundraisers around the world. As you'd expect, in amongst this book's practical tips, rants, keys and big ideas 'How to love your donors (to death)', covers all the basic essentials of fundraising direct marketing and also throws in some sensible insights into the more complex aspects of this endlessly fascinating activity. Its pages are packed with sound advice on everything from how to communicate effectively and responsibly to how to maximise return on investment and while at it, how to enjoy the process too. Step by step Stephen guides you through the intricacies of his chosen field, illuminating its quirkiness and shining light into its gloomier recesses while sharing shedloads of secrets, stories and insights that will help you both to raise lots more money cost-effectively and to feel satisfied while you do it of the rightness of your approach. He even helps you get your grammar right.

Many of the gems in this book are deliciously straightforward and simple. Stephen exhorts fundraisers to be less demanding and more engaging, a simple recipe that in itself could transform fundraising, or at least the donor experience of it, overnight.

We should all join forces to campaign for a transformation of the donor experience, yet sadly only a tiny, privileged elite of readers will take this book's advice to heart. Their organisations and causes will prosper accordingly. Fundraising I'm sure will increasingly divide into those who get this and those who don't. This book therefore is for fundraisers with the vision, tenacity and campaigning zeal not just to change the world but to change the way fundraising is done, not only in their organisation but throughout our sector. Causes in future will be increasingly categorised as those that do great fundraising, and those that don't. As you're holding this book in your hands, you have made a good start.

Ken Burnett,
London
2nd October 2014.

CONTENTS

1 Why should you be reading this?

I am a fundraiser, my medium is direct marketing and my audience is Minor Donors – good people who give ordinary donations. I speak at conferences all over the world on this sort of fundraising. And as I get older and become part of the population segment that is most likely to donate, I feel more and more abused by charities trying to squeeze the last penny out of me. It's madness, because people like me – and there are millions of us – need to be loved by charities… loved to death!

Loving your donors is a strategy with high returns. The money donated during their lifetime through small donations is but a drop in the ocean. If a charity provides a supporter with a consistent and happy experience, then when they die they will leave a legacy. And the value of that gift will eclipse all the donations they gave in their life.

That's the subject of this book. I'll show you how to do it and, in one or two of my 'rants', how not to do it. Everything in this book is designed to leave the supporter feeling appreciated, 'loved' in my terms. But I have to start with some fundamentals of fundraising – one fact and two phenomena.

Lots of people give to charities and if you're reading this, I'll guarantee you're one of them. But serious money comes from people who are older than you. That's just a fact of life – people who are over 60 are more wealthy, a lot more wealthy. The figures from the Office of National Statistics in the UK released in 2014[1] are very clear. Wealth in this report has four constituent parts: property wealth; financial wealth (cash, savings, stocks etc.); physical wealth (the mass of things you own); and private

1 Wealth and Assets Survey (2014) 'Wealth in Great Britain 2010/12'. Office for National Statistics, London. www.ons.gov.uk/ons/dcp171776_362809.pdf

pension wealth. In these terms, three categories of people stand out a mile – all of them are 'older'. They are over pensionable age, or couples with one partner over pensionable age, or couples with children who are no longer dependent. That's no surprise; it simply confirms the social structures we've lived with for years.

And the age of 'around 60' neatly coincides with two other life-changing phenomena. If you haven't experienced them, you cannot know how immensely liberating, how truly amazing they are.

The first is retirement. Throughout countless years of work, people have relied on you, you've had responsibilities, whatever your level in the organisation. When you are working, you have obligations. When you retire, all that goes. It's wonderful; I recommend it to everyone I now meet. I've never worked so hard in my life, but the responsibilities I had, the obligations to colleagues, have virtually disappeared.

The second phenomenon for most people is that children leave home, not just to go to university or whatever, but to set up somewhere on their own. While that may bring some element of sadness, it also signals an amazing sense of freedom.

Not only do older people have more money, but retirement and the children leaving home encourage a new view of life, liberated from responsibilities to others at work and from the concentration of all energies on raising the family.

In this book you will learn a huge amount about Minor Donor fundraising – raising smaller gifts from lots of people, often through a regular monthly donation paid through their bank. But it is not about techniques – the detail of recruitment or media or testing or what software to use for an email campaign. Nor do I laboriously debate the merits of digital versus paper fundraising. This stuff is monumentally boring and has been clogging up conference sessions for the last decade without achieving the fundamental shift needed in fundraisers – the change in their attitude to the wonderful folk who support their cause.

This book is about how to love your donors. As anyone knows, falling in love is easy, but loving somebody over time, though a joy, is also hard work. Loving your donors requires a fundamental shift in attitude, a long-term strategy and a strong commitment to getting it right. Creating great experiences together is a huge part of the work of loving.

The principles outlined by legendary copywriter George Smith in 'Asking Properly', and articulated so clearly by UK fundraising guru Ken Burnett in 'Relationship Fundraising', have guided fundraisers for 20 years. Don't you just love the word 'properly'? It is so very English, and has bound up in it all the good things I learned as a boy, and none of the bad. For fundraisers throughout the world, the word describes perfectly how supporters should be treated – properly. Treating Minor Donors properly means honouring them, involving their emotions and appreciating their commitment over the years. It is understood in principle, but in practice very few charities have strategies to deliver that care. Many pay lip service to it. Some, the best, are outstanding beacons in Minor Donor fundraising. However, most charities continue to pursue fundraising techniques with both eyes firmly fixed on the target income figure set for the year.

So why a book now? Well, three reasons. The first is that falling response rates in most media have unsettled many fundraisers and encouraged them to abandon the basic principle: 'People give to people, not to charities'. Talking about the work of your charity is boring; talking about how the donor's gift will transform a life somewhere… that is still the stuff of wonder! So this book takes you back to absolute basics: who is supporting your charity, why are they doing it, and how you could be making their giving a truly rewarding experience?

My second reason for writing is this. In the huge rush of excitement to go digital, the old techniques are being at best ignored, and at worst, despised. A couple of years ago I was debating with an American online fundraising guru on the proposal that direct mail would be replaced by online methods in five years. He didn't believe it any more than I did but, at one point, he turned on me: 'Stephen, I can tell you that in New York, people of my age (he was in his thirties) never even open their post boxes'. I didn't respond; I'd been rude enough already expressing my contempt for the proposal. But the reality is that the money raised from people his age is dwarfed by that from older generations, which explains why online fundraising in 2013 still brought in less than 7% of charitable income for US charities[2].

2 Blackbaud (2013) 'Charitable Giving Report 2013'. www.blackbaud.com/nonprofit-resources/charitablegiving see chapter 11

The trouble is, supporters are taking second place to the techniques available to reach them. They are being abused more systematically now than they have been for 20 years, with fundraisers diverted to focus on the latest jazzy e-newsletter or clever website campaign. Just experience the process for yourself. Sign up on- or offline to a pile of charities and start making monthly payments to them through the bank. The experience with some is a joy. Most are a disaster!

The third reason for writing is probably the most worrying of all. Public opinion, traditionally and strongly in support of charities, is by no means secure. The public, in the UK at least, is all too ready to criticise charities for face-to-face street fundraising, the salaries of senior staff and half a dozen other gripes. Actually, the percentage of complaints is a miniscule proportion of the vast number of contacts charities have with the public in any year. What other sector in our society would receive a note from a customer pointing out their name on a mailing had been spelt wrong, record that as a 'complaint' and list it with other complaints in the annual return to the 'complaints' body, the Fundraising Standards Board? That's what happens in the UK, where the charity sector is incredibly transparent.

As a trustee of the Institute of Fundraising for six years, the nearest thing UK fundraisers have to a 'governing body', I had the interesting task of chairing the Standards Committee that created and now maintains the Code of Practice, which sets the standards for fundraising in the UK. These standards are some of the highest in the world and are maintained at that level by volunteers sitting on vetting committees and fundraisers taking them very seriously. I am immensely proud of our sector.

But clear standards are not enough. This book will encourage you to change your view of your donors, to be less demanding and more engaging. Long-term thinking requires effort of course, but that effort will be rewarded many times over by higher and long-term income for your charity. Let me encourage your change of view with some startling figures.

I am indebted to The Royal British Legion for allowing me to show you figures that should completely transform the way you love your donors. The Legion's campaign to grow its database of supporters significantly began in the early 2000s and particularly in 2004, the 60th anniversary of the D-Day landings in France. Every year, solid investment was made in supporter recruitment.

Recruitment Year	Supporters	Legacy Value (£)
2002	174	3,248,899
2003	144	1,454,007
2004	152	2,260,210
2005	131	2,219,724
2006	58	716,993
2007	43	555,745
2008	70	914,379
2009	77	1,110,061
2010	37	332,582
2011	20	212,165
2012	11	942,772
2014	1	1,000

New supporters leaving a legacy by year of recruitment
by kind permission of The Royal British Legion

The figures show the numbers of new supporters, recruited via cold activity (direct mail, doordrops and inserts) by year of recruitment, that have subsequently died and left a gift in their Wills. The total value so far from these 12 years of recruitment is a little short of £14 million. That is over and above the ongoing, profitable income these new supporters had given in the years since their first gift.

And these are only the 'figures so far'; it's a snapshot taken at a point in time. When, in another 12 years, a fundraiser looks back at the equivalent set of figures, they may see legacy income from those recruited in 2014 at £3.3 million and still continuing to rise? Guy Upward, responsible for all Minor Donor fundraising and the architect of the spectacular growth of the Legion's active database, made a comment that should be echoed throughout the sector: 'I always look at the return on investment when reviewing new supporters generated from cold. I obviously need to look at these figures too, as nearly £14 million in 'incremental' income is not too shabby, is it?'

If you knew that good stewardship is more likely to lead to a gift in a supporter's Will, then practically any cost would be considered a smart investment. But you do know, instinctively, that honouring donors, treating them 'properly', builds their loyalty.

There are two key conclusions from these figures that should, by right, revise all fundraising strategy. If the value of legacies is included in lifetime value calculations, then the allowable cost of recruitment (particularly of older people) can rise. Secondly, the serious investment of money to steward the best donors can be viewed as the smartest investment available.

A new strategy would be born; recruit as many older people to support your charity as possible and, when you've done that, invest smart money to make them appreciate how very much you rely on and value their support. Of course this requires a long-term view of a charity's income and expenditure. But who was it who ever convinced charity trustees that their sole requirement was to agree a one-year income strategy? No-one, but this has become the norm with so-called five-year strategies no better than a series of one-year strategies thrown together to make it look like they are planning ahead. They are not, most trustees are shamefully neglecting their duty. Or maybe fundraisers are distracted by the excitements of the new and exciting and have not yet made their view clear and unassailable that short-term fundraising targets achieve a lot less than a long-term strategy.

No more than a handful of charities have ever taken investment in legacy marketing seriously. Look at how few charities have ever asked for legacies on TV; in the UK, hardly any. Yet the cost of a strong television campaign would be covered by no more than five or six legacies. But that money may not come in for eight or ten years, yet in the terms of the longevity of most charities, that's practically tomorrow. The boards and senior management of most charities do not look beyond one year; it is a complete travesty.

In the next chapter I begin a series of ideas that deliver great stewardship; a way to make donors feel loved and appreciated.

2 Getting the supporter experience right

I t is the fundraiser's job, your only job, to make the supporter feel good about supporting your charity. You have to love your donors. The money will follow.

Think about the quality of the experience you give to your supporters. Better still, what do you feel about your own experience as a supporter when you donate to other charities? You do donate to other charities, don't you? You do watch what they do to follow up your donation and ask you to support them further? Frankly, if you are not giving to all your immediate competitors to test their systems, you are missing a trick. You learn such a lot from this tactic.

What do you feel about the way the charities you support actually treat you? I donate to many of the best fundraising charities in the UK and have done for years. What is my experience? Do I feel 'recognised' or 'cared for', for instance? **Not in the slightest.** Most treat me with studied indifference and far too many send me a never-ending stream of boring letters, emails, and demands for money or a slice of my Will.

Is the fundraising sector any different from commerce? Sadly, I now think it is far worse. Let me tell you a story from the commercial sector 15 years ago. My mother died and left my brother and me a lump of money. It was the sort of sum that would change life a bit and there were lots of temptations to spend it all. But, astonishingly, my wife and I decided not to blow it on a new car, holiday and the pile of stuff the kids suggested, but we did the thing my mother would most have wanted. We used it to pay off a chunk of the loan on our house.

Feeling positively virtuous, we sent a cheque to the company that supplied the loan, the Cheltenham & Gloucester Building Society, and sat back to receive congratulations. After a long time, we received a letter from a Mr Watkin, Mortgage Advisor. Such a stiff, pompous letter. Mr Watkin barely acknowledged the large sum we had sent him, but seemed to take pleasure in reminding us that, as some of the mortgage was still outstanding, the Society would continue to hold the deeds of our house until it was paid off. With that letter, the balance of power had been restored; we had been reminded that, still, we did not own our house and that we were in debt to the building society.

I felt cheated. I knew I had been sensible, but of course, my mother was no longer there to say 'well done, my boy' as no doubt she would have done. My sense of annoyance was directed at the Cheltenham & Gloucester Building Society, of which Mr. Watkin was simply a servant. There, I've again been able to remind you of the name of the company that gave me such displeasure!

This was the same company that spent millions of pounds on television every year telling the world what a wonderful mortgage provider it was. I beg to differ. My experience was very different from the expensive advertising. And when a few years later I needed a bigger house and a bigger mortgage to match my bigger children, the Cheltenham & Gloucester Building Society (there, I've said it again!) was very definitely not on my list of potential lenders.

I am sure you could match this story with one of your own – stories of poor experience at the hands of an unthinking company. However, in recent years commercial companies have fallen over themselves trying to improve the 'customer experience'. There are literally thousands of books on the subject. And some companies are transforming the way they do business. Customer Experience Directors are appearing on main boards, Customer Experience Statements are being issued and so on.

I am reminded of a quotation from Beverley Hodson, then Managing Director of the high street chain W H Smith: 'Customer experience is the reality of the brand'. A company can say what it likes in its advertising, but the real brand is how its customers view it.

Are any of these efforts reflected in our fundraising sector? Virtually none. I have seen little evidence of mailings, emails or telephone calls that are remotely responsive to the interests of specific groups of Minor Donors. Few reflect the relationship indicated by the donor's response or lack of it to any proposition. Nearly three decades after we started talking about real, responsive, innovative supporter care, very few UK charities are doing it yet. Several are investing a lot of money towards achieving that goal, so things may improve in the future. And there are individual examples of good practice, of course. Dogs Trust, for instance, seems to hit the spot perfectly with those wanting a virtual relationship with a dog. It truly understands its supporters, but sadly, very few other charities are doing this.

Why are most supporter experiences so poor? There are several reasons. Fundraisers have only a certain amount of energy, and the message from the board of trustees is clear – 'Make your budget first, then we'll worry about that other clever stuff later'. With fundraisers organised by function – different people responsible for the recruitment of cash donors, for regular monthly givers or legacies, for instance – their focus is to hit the income target for their individual campaigns. As a result, few charities are looking after their supporters anywhere near as well as they could. The result is that relationships are eroded, opportunities pass unnoticed and, in the end, budgets are not actually achieved. The irony is that the strategy of subjecting individual supporters to mass mailings, mass email campaigns and badly scripted telephone calls is not even working.

This stuff is not difficult, but it requires people with a passion for good supporter care, people who see the long-term benefit of asking for supporters' opinions and feedback, people whose raison d'être is to develop ongoing, mutually beneficial and hence profitable relationships. And they must have the strong backing of senior management.

I like the concept of stewardship. The Steward was employed to look after the traditional estate, to nurture it and make it profitable. The job of the fundraiser is very similar – you're there to nurture your supporters, to love them, to make them feel really good about their giving. The money will come later.

Stephen's rant 1

Fundraisers the world-over know the impact on a charity's senior management team of the whiff of a major donation. Senior managers start to salivate, with some expressing crass views that Major Donor fundraising is the most important source of the charity's money.

Depending on the number of 0's on the gift, the Chief Executive will make sure he or she is available at strategically important times. The Head of Service Provision or Science or whatever the cause may be, is warned they may have to explain the need for substantial funds and they are delighted to help out. Contrast this response to the attitude of senior management towards most small donors – Minor Donors. At best, studied indifference. At worst, dislike, disinterest in providing any information that might please them, unwillingness to meet them, and demands that money should be extracted from them at least cost. There are many senior staff in charities who actually find the whole business of asking for money distinctly grubby. Their view, that it is begging, shames them and I curse their ignorant arrogance.

And yet, many of these Minor Donors could leave a gift in their Will that could transcend all but the biggest gifts from the wealthiest Major Donors.

*By virtue of being around since the early days, I confess, with shame, to being one of the early protagonists of our current strategy – the more you ask, the more you get. I remember the excitement in the mid-1980s at the income we generated every time we went out with an appeal. Failing to ask for money seemed indecent at the time. And of course, at its baldest, it is right – the more you ask, the more you **do** get. But, with so many charities now doing it, through so many media, 'the more you ask' means the more supporters feel hounded.*

*I remember a couple of years ago participating in a long-running and tense blog on the subject of 'Should the thank-you letter contain another clear ask for money'? Both sides were adamant, with the pro-lobby pretty well saying a fundraiser is in dereliction of their duty if they don't ask every time they write. In my opinion, **that is plain wrong.** You're less likely to get a legacy from a supporter who you've* *consistently upset by not recognising their personal giving preferences. How you do that, how you 'love your donors', starts with how you improve the stewardship of your supporters and how you make them feel fantastic about their favourite charity,* **your** *charity.*

In the next three chapters I explore the whole area of the supporter experience, offer dozens of ideas on how to improve the way you relate to your donors, and explore what stewardship could really look like if done properly.

3 What builds supporter loyalty?

What is good stewardship? Let me start with four key factors that come from research done in 2004 and 2005 for my fundraising agency, Target Direct. We were looking at ways to build 'supporter loyalty' and commissioned research into its key drivers. The research was carried out by my colleague and friend Adrian Sargeant, now Professor of Fundraising at the University of Plymouth, together with Elaine Jay, a skilled and practical fundraiser.

We wanted to isolate the key things a charity can do to convert supporters from what Adrian and Elaine call 'passive supporters' to 'active supporters'. In this context, 'active' and 'passive' describe not whether they have given a donation recently – you can have a 'passive supporter' who is making a monthly donation through the bank – but how a supporter feels about the charity they are supporting: whether they feel close, interested, even warm, or distant, un-involved but still giving support.

The research highlights the factors that distinguish between the two. Four elements clearly improve 'active support' – information, campaigning, telephone contact and research.

3.1 Information

It comes as no surprise that supporters enjoy receiving information about the work of their favoured charity and, specifically, about the impact their support, their donation, has made on that work. I could name dozens of charities that do this brilliantly.

For example, The Royal British Legion sends out a super supporters' magazine three times a year, called 'Poppy Press'. The Legion is the UK's largest charity for people who have been in the Armed Services and, in England and Wales, is responsible for the annual Poppy Day celebrations in November. In the mid-1990s The Legion was in definite decline; now, because of its huge investment in fundraising since that time, it is an immensely successful charity. It succeeded in re-instating the two-minute silence of remembrance at 11am on the 11th day of the 11th month – the exact time of the end of the First World War – which is now observed by a very high percentage of British people.

'Poppy Press' gives information. It simply describes the impact of the work of The Legion as seen through the eyes of the ex-service folk in its care. This work is paid for by the donations of supporters and the magazine is beautifully crafted to link donors with what it achieves. There is the softest of 'asks' in the letter that comes with the magazine, yet the mailing regularly raises a seven-figure sum in pounds sterling.

A charity magazine is a basic tool of the fundraiser's trade, but some still manage to get it wrong. Don't make it too glossy, and only report what is being achieved with the supporters' money. Don't include stories of small sums of money raised in obscure places with a picture of the smiling folk who did it. They are the only ones interested and it makes your charity sound so parochial.

Stephen's rant 2

The supporter magazine is one of my pet hates. There is nothing wrong with a good magazine – it's a great medium for delivering information to the generation that sends the most donations. But most charities get it wrong. Too often magazines are produced by the communications department rather than the fundraising department. Why does this happen? Mostly, it's the result of a power struggle between communications and fundraising, which the former wins because chief executives like communications departments; they feel communications can contribute to the charity's marketing without having to deal with the less glamorous (indeed, grubby) business of fundraising.

Secondly, many magazines are written by staff with English degrees, people who were never journalists, so never learned the art of written communication. The writing skills they apply are those learned at university or school and there is no-one skilled enough in charities to throw their copy back at them for a re-write in simple colloquial English; English that connects. Ask yourself why the retail magazine sector is so successful – it's because the writing is sublime, the design flawless and the pictures arresting. And the stories they tell are about people – gossip really. Most charity magazines are like reports for the Chief Executive. The pictures are so small you can't see anything, space is used as a substitute for good design (because that is what the designer was taught in year one of art college), and there is very little content worth reading.

As for those charities producing four or even six supporter magazines a year, my contention is that it is a complete waste of time and money, though it does justify a full-time job for the editor. The first thing a fundraiser should do is ask for an independent readership survey. Unless the magazine is exceptional, the readership will be low. It is not therefore achieving its job of getting information on the impact of their gifts to a substantial proportion of the donors.

I've seen magazines from charities that look virtually identical, just different colours. It's because many use the same cheap, do-it-yourself software packages. Disaster…do they not realise that supporters give donations to other charities as well as their own?

Producing two or, possibly, three magazines a year shows a determination to tell the donor about the impact of their gifts and sets a structure for the communication. The 'ask' in these magazines should be very soft. The magazines show the supporter you want to give them feedback.

But there are other, more effective ways to get your information out. What about a simple photocopy of an important report that's just arrived on the Chief Executive's desk? Or perhaps a wonderful picture that would warm the hearts of all the supporters, with a note simply saying: 'I thought you would enjoy this picture of the kids on the holiday that your donation made possible'. Just think of the smile on the supporter's face when they open that note from you.

Practical tips 1

How can a fundraiser produce information that feels 'special'? One of the best examples I've seen is a mailing from the UK charity Sense, which supports people with hearing and sight impairment. In it, three pages duplicated from the magazine of the country's highest selling broadsheet newspaper tell the story of a deaf-blind woman achieving amazing things. The feature gives information like any charity magazine article, but it's well written with good graphics. What makes it special is the compliments slip that comes with it from Lee Green. The words are clever: 'Dear Mr. Pidgeon, in case you didn't see it, I'm sending you a copy of a rather wonderful article that appeared recently in the Telegraph Magazine'. The compliments slip makes me feel as though Mr Green has thought of me personally. And that makes me feel like a million dollars.

That's an example of **real** communication; it really connects me with the impact my gift is having on an actual person who is both deaf and blind. But real communication needs a whole new way of thinking.

I've watched fundraisers as they interact with supporters on Facebook or Twitter – light-hearted, fun, quite personal conversations. Brilliant. But they're dealing with no more than a handful of supporters. In fact, many of these people don't even donate. Yet, rightly, the charity is prepared to allow the fundraiser time to do that.

The skills that fundraisers practise when they're in their own natural medium (Facebook or Twitter) need to be applied to the tens or hundreds of thousands of real donors on your database. Don't ignore them because they are old, or were recruited the 'old fashioned way', by mail. Treat them in the same intimate way; they'll love it. Simple steps to take include:

- Highlight the top 20% of supporters by value simply by analysing your income from each, less the costs of maintaining that support, remembering to factor in how long they have supported you – recent donors will not have had time to build value yet

- Send these supporters only one, possibly two, magazines per year

• But send two or three further 'personal' communications, such as:

- a short report with a hand-written message on a compliments slip (of course the slip is printed but make it really look like it's handwritten, complete with marks or even splodges of ink)

- a story that you heard at work that really made you feel proud to be working for your charity

- a card at Christmas summarising the charity's successful (or challenging) year.

Stephen's rant 3

There are signs that the horror that is the monthly charity e-newsletter is beginning to change. It cannot do so quickly enough.

Email is the most flexible, individual medium that's ever been available to fundraisers. It has immense potential to deliver engaging information. Yet if you sign up to all but the most innovative charities, you receive emails that are crushingly boring.

For a start, they break every rule ever established for direct marketing – and email is a direct marketing medium. Each email looks the same: text-heavy, in the same format with only the date being changed. Every email lists the headlines of articles that are then accessed through the website. But the headlines simply don't engage my imagination, and if I click through I am faced with a column of type that is unexciting to read on a subject that is not of my choosing.

The fundamental problem is the assumption that supporters are desperate to read about the things that fundraisers want to talk about. They're not. Every time an e-newsletter goes out, it has to do a very difficult job. It has to excite the supporter so much that opening it is a 'must do' experience. So, for a start, don't send one every month. Few will be opened and most are intensely irritating to receive. Put more effort into sending 'occasional' emails that really engage. Personalise them by bringing to the front the stories that have in the past prompted me to give money. In the subject box use the word you – 'News just in, Stephen, of the children you are helping with your kind gifts'. And fill them with pictures and video and exciting things that show me why I'm so smart to be supporting your charity.

3.2 Campaigning

The second activity that distinguishes an 'active supporter' from a 'passive supporter' is their involvement in campaigning.

Campaigning is the natural role for a number of successful non-profits – Greenpeace, Friends of the Earth and Amnesty International are just three. It's a major part of their existence. Indeed, for many of them, getting someone to take part in an activity is the best way to recruit them later into a donating relationship. Their conversion, perhaps to making a regular monthly gift through their bank, comes in a subsequent telephone call where the success or otherwise of the campaign is an easy opening topic of discussion.

For anyone to campaign for an organisation shows a commitment, a meeting of values, that is highly likely, long-term, to lead to a donation. In a long list of superb campaigns from these three organisations, one of the best appeared at the end of 2012. I saw it on the London Underground and was blown away. It said: 'A man presses send at Paddington Station and a stoning is stopped in Iran'. My text message was on its way moments after I reached street level.

For other charities, Christian Aid, RSPCA (the UK's biggest animal charity) and World Horse Welfare, for instance, campaigning has been used partly as a way of increasing the impact of their message to governments and partly to strengthen the bond with their supporters. As a tactic to get close to your supporters, there is nothing more successful than campaigning.

The reasons are obvious. Anyone who feels passionately enough to sign a petition, write to their member of parliament or send an email, feels good when they've done it (and even better when they receive a reply). It singles them out as someone who 'cares' enough to bother.

Yet there are many campaigning charities where fundraising and campaigning are run completely separately. It usually comes about when both sides get territorial about 'their' supporters. Lunacy! The supporters are the charity's supporters – they don't distinguish between the departments writing to them. These are immensely valuable, long-term believers in the charity and highly likely to leave a legacy when they die. The trouble is, they will die decades later when the warring parties that were determined never to work together and share their databases have long since disappeared.

Practical tips 2

You need to know who these people are. Make sure you record any campaigning action they do for you. If you want them to send a letter to their MP, make sure they send it to you first. There are two reasons for this: you can compile many letters together and present them to Parliament but, more importantly, you'll know who on your database is really fired up with your values, and sufficiently committed to write a letter of support. You can then upgrade their status on your database to that of donor **and** campaigner – a much more valuable beast. If it's an email, get them to copy you in. Texts, record their activity. Then, whatever the medium, you can keep them in touch with the outcome of their action as well as thanking them for backing your campaign.

Your job is to make them feel good about their interaction with your charity, to make their experience the very best it can be. And campaigning is an exciting and rewarding experience if it's handled well.

3.3 Phone calls

Research in 2012 by the authoritative US fundraising guru Penelope Burk and Chuck Longfield, analysis doyen of US database company Blackbaud, shows that if you phone to thank a new cash supporter for their gift, simply phone to say: 'Thank you' with no further 'ask', then the money you'll get from them in the following year will increase by an average of 40%. Imagine it, you'd get 40% more from supporters, simply by phoning to thank them for their first gift. And these are some of the nicest calls, both to make and receive. Even if you put the task out to an agency, the increased value would give you a return on investment of three or four to one. You can read about it on the Showcase of Fundraising Innovation and Inspiration (SOFII)[3].

The research relates to direct mail. Similar figures for other recruitment media emerged recently from one of the UK's best telephone fundraising agencies, Pell & Bales. I recommend you read Bethan Holloway's definitive piece entitled 'How to reduce donor attrition by a third in 3 minutes'[4]. The title says it all. Pell & Bales' researchers found that a simple phone call expressing welcome and thanks reduced attrition rates for face-to-face, door-to-door and cold telemarketing recruits by between 30% and 40%. These are such significant numbers, every Minor Donor fundraiser should be looking to test these ideas. You're mad if you don't.

The phone is an immensely valuable fundraising tool, often derided by people who should know better. I support many charities so I am regularly phoned at home. Without exception, these calls are interesting, engaging, charmingly delivered… everything you'd want from a good fundraiser! The ones I like the most thank me for my recent support and update me on the impact my donation or regular monthly gift is having. The best allow me to go off-script and ask questions about the work – and I can only do that if the caller is bright and has been well briefed by the charity. Most are brilliant at it.

Short of actually meeting the supporter, the phone is the most intimate medium available to the fundraiser. It can help to develop the relationship with supporters and build 'active support'. Used well, it is a huge asset. Used badly, the infection quickly spreads to the whole of the charity sector, not just that charity. In the UK at least, it is well regulated, with the ever-present threat of the Telephone Preference

3 Chuck's article is at www.sofii.org/node/1181
4 Blog (2012) http://pellandbales.wordpress.com/2012/08/15/how-to-reduce-donor-attrition-by-a-third-in-3-minutes

Service, through which anybody can ban calls. Currently, over 15 million people are signed up to the Service to prevent non-solicited phone calls to their home or mobile phones – that's a lot of people who have been put off receiving phone calls.

3.4 Research

Asking people for their views is a sure way to build 'active support', according to the Sargeant and Jay research mentioned at the beginning of this chapter. People love to give their opinions, it is integral to the spirit of philanthropy. As a donor, and provided the 'ask' is not too difficult to deliver, you are happy to 'help out' in any way you can.

Think about it; a charity whose work you admire writes to you asking for your views. This is a charity you have supported with, probably, several donations. You like what it is trying to achieve and the way it sets about its work.

Now ask yourself how you would feel if the charity tells you that your views could help in its fundraising or even in deciding the priorities on different aspects of its work. You would be thrilled to give your views, pleased that you had been asked. And tests have shown that this pleasure is translated into further and more committed support in subsequent appeals.

Careful questionnaires seeking the views and experiences of supporters can produce valuable information. They can be delivered through paper and matched online, giving the supporter an alternative way of responding. What questions should it ask? For medical charities, what experience does the supporter have of the illness? For overseas development, which countries/continents interest them and why? Which aspects of the development work are most interesting? For animal charities, what animals does the supporter have? All this information can be used in subsequent fundraising.

For many years in the 1990s and 2000s, many of the big fundraising charities in the UK sought donations using questionnaires as a means of cold recruitment. They were effective at producing donations at a reasonable cost. Sadly, most charities ignored the information returned to them, confirming my view that the questionnaires were merely a device to get a response. Subsequently, the Standards Committee of the Institute of Fundraising tightened its standard of good fundraising practice and required charities to data capture at least a representative sample of the responses.

Take the RSPCA, the UK's biggest animal charity. In the mid-1990s, a question in its cold recruitment questionnaire mailing asked whether the supporter had a dog or a cat. For an animal charity whose subsequent appeals would be based mostly on cases of cruelty to either dogs or cats, it was an obvious question. But the RSPCA didn't even data capture this information, claiming it had tested its subsequent use and found it worthless. I do not believe it. In my view it should have asked for the names of the supporter's pets, loading all that information onto the supporter's file and using it in subsequent appeals.

But the real importance of research is not in the information your kind supporters are pleased to give you. It lies in two facts – that you have expressed an interest in hearing the supporter's views and that they have responded by giving them. The latter shows their support is much more likely to be 'active' than 'passive'.

Practical tips 3

One of the best mailings I have ever seen was from Guide Dogs. This excellent charity relies on legacies for about 50% of its income each year. So the mailing told its supporters of the charity's intention to start advertising for new people who would be prepared to leave it a gift in their Will. It included four possible advertisements and asked the supporter to read each one, grading them on how likely they were to get someone to leave a legacy. Brilliant.

The mailing asked supporters for their views and we already know that research builds 'active' support. No doubt, all the supporters chosen to receive the mailing were old – the very market for the advertisements – so their views would be a good indication of the likely subsequent response from a similar audience. But, most of all, the elderly supporters read four advertisements asking for a gift in their

Will. At the end of that, these good people, supporters of Guide Dogs probably for many years, would have understood the message and taken it to heart – the charity relies heavily on legacies for its work. Job done.

Stephen's rant 4

Now a less good experience. Practical Action, an interesting overseas aid charity I had supported for many years, wrote to me a few years ago saying that, if I were agreeable, a research company would call to hear my views on its work. It was a favourite charity of mine and I was pleased to be able to help in this way. But I never heard from the research company.

*Finally, I re-read the letter and noticed, right at the bottom, a paragraph saying if I didn't hear by a certain date, it would mean the research was complete. The charity had told me it wanted my views but in the end, hadn't bothered to call me. I felt completely let down. In fact, I was annoyed. My experience had now become wholly **negative**.*

How unnecessary, how very foolish of Practical Action. It could easily have sent me a letter, explaining the researchers had tried but been unable to contact me. It could have given me a simple summary of the findings of the research, perhaps inviting me to write back if I disagreed. This would have kept me engaged – simple to do, but requiring a new way of thinking about supporters and the relationship needed with them.

The Practical Action fundraisers were at best thoughtless. They wanted information and devised a means to obtain it. At no time did they consider the other side of this relationship between the charity and its supporter. I was left angry.

As fundraisers, we have to stop thinking like this. The basic reason so many people report bad experiences in dealing with the charities they support is because fundraisers do not see their job as creating good experiences for their supporters.

Most see it as persuading donors to give them money. It doesn't work that way. It used to, but it doesn't now.

In the next chapter, I offer four more areas to make the supporter's experience of your charity more rewarding. Rewarding experiences will always, in the end, lead to more money, and could result in a legacy gift.

4 Thinking differently

These ideas to improve the experience you give your supporters (and a host of practical tips to go with them) have one thing in common; you have to start thinking differently. If you find this difficult, try to remember one of the most important 'truths' of fundraising: 'Nobody is interested in what you do'. At conferences I've seen fundraisers flinch at this bold assertion. It's as if I have denied everything they've stood for in their working life.

Fundraisers **love** to describe their charity's wonderful work, the detail of what happens in the field or laboratory, what my small gift will buy if I donate, how their staff colleagues are organised to deliver the work, and so on. **Nobody** is interested in any of it; nobody is interested in what the charity does. They are only interested in what happens when that work is done, the outcome of the work, its impact on patients, poor people, animals or whatever is the subject of your cause.

The moment you understand this simple fundraising truth, your results will begin to improve. You will become less obsessed with your own charity and more understanding of your supporter. Your thinking will change. You will write differently when you are putting together your appeals, website or fundraising literature. I will develop these ideas further in Chapter 9 when I explore the whole area of delivering creative messages.

4.1 Understanding the complexity of giving

I have been fascinated over recent years by the work of my colleagues Professors Adrian Sargeant and Jen Shang at the University of Indiana[5] seeking to quantify the

---

5 Sargeant A. and Shang J. (2010). 'Fundraising Principles and Practice'. Jossey Bass, San Francisco.

impact of a person's own 'identity' on their desire to donate. This challenging research was started by Jen Shang in 2007, when she was working with America's Public Broadcasting Service (PBS). If you are looking for consistently good, educational, intelligent broadcasting in the US, you are likely to watch or listen to your local PBS station. These stations (some 800 all together) are ubiquitous and, with the early ones set up in the 1950s and 1960s, they rely for a large proportion of their income on support from the listeners and viewers in their catchment areas.

As a result, a whole industry of fundraising from ordinary viewers and listeners has grown up over the years. It is quintessentially the American way of supporting vital public services. Most of the public libraries are funded this way as well. It's incredibly impressive to non-Americans like me.

The fundraising starts on-air and supporters phone in to begin or renew their yearly membership subscription. Looking at what might prompt a higher gift, researchers manipulated the telephone scripts dealing with these calls to see the impact of what they called 'social information'. Here's an illustration. In a control group of those donating for the first time, viewers and listeners were asked to make their 'annual gift'; they chose the value with no prompt. Those in the test group however, were told, just before the 'ask': 'We've just had another member who has just contributed $xxx, how much would you like to give'? Three different sums were tested – $75, $180, $300. In the control group, the average membership was $86.58. The averages in the test groups were respectively $87.44, $96.98 and $111.91.

It was a simple experiment with a simple outcome. Told that 'another member' had just contributed a higher gift, new members raised their contribution – significantly.

The same happened with members who were renewing. Naming a value of $300, for instance, increased the average subscription by $26.47. Interestingly, the researchers found that one year later (without prompts) members continued to renew their subscription on the phone at their higher rates.

These experiments were designed to be definitive. For the technically minded, there was an interesting conclusion on the optimum value to ask for. Given the early results, which showed that the higher the figure named, the more you got, it was tempting to name a supporter who had just given a $1,000 gift. In most cases that didn't work and the researchers showed that the 'optimum' value to ask for fell between the 90th and the 95th percentile of established gift values. Their advice was to rank all values in a continuum, divide that continuum into 'appropriate' segments, then ask members of that segment for the value between the 90th and the 95th percentile of the segment. But that's a lot of detail.

In ethical terms, of course, you could only name a gift value that had been given already by a supporter, so the experiment was not entirely controllable.

Interestingly, all the above experimentation worked equally in direct mail renewal as well as telephone renewal.

So then the researchers got cute. The challenge was that by naming the value of a gift, the researchers were doing nothing more than prompting a value, in the same way that a row of tick box values on an appeal donation form prompts higher gifts. So they changed the script. Just before the 'ask', they gave the Christian name of the member who had made the gift: 'We've just had another member Mary, who has contributed $300, how much would you like to give Stephen'? They found that where the gender of the named member was matched with that of the new or renewing member, the increase in their gift was significantly higher than when the genders were mis-matched, as they are in the above example.

What on earth is going on here? The argument is that making a donation to a charity is much more emotionally significant than simply sending off some money. Donating involves the supporter's very 'identity'. When, for instance, callers were asked to estimate the number of their friends who listened to the radio station, the higher the number named, the higher was the average gift subsequently given; there was a direct correlation. The supporters could not possibly know how many of their friends listened to that radio station, so the naming of a high number had to be more to do with their view of themselves, their 'identity'.

Research such as this will, one day, change the way we treat our donors. Making a donation is not simply a transaction. It is fundamental to how supporters see themselves in the context of their 'society' and we ignore that at our peril.

4.2 Thanking people

We've already seen from the Longfield research how thanking someone by phone for their first cash gift increased donations by 40%. And it is now widely established practice that a thank-you letter is an essential element of the process of getting closer to the donor. But, in places I visit round the world, this concept is still questioned and there are even UK charities deciding to thank only those people who send more than, say, £100.

That is outrageous. It's probable that the £100 gift is considerably less of a sacrifice than the £5 gift from a pensioner. And, as most gifts (still) come from people aged more than 60 who were brought up in a more gracious age, then 'thanks' is a requirement. Sure, it costs a bit, but there are two key reasons to do it.

Firstly, it's a great excuse to go back to the supporter, offer a little more information about how their gift is being used to change lives and renew the inner pleasure they felt when they were moved enough by your story to send you a gift. But the second reason is much more significant. While each gift is a valuable contribution to funds whatever its size, it is the giving of the gift that is the real value.

Several pieces of research within charities have shown that those who give donations, or time, or purchase gifts from the catalogue, or buy raffle tickets, are more likely to leave a gift in their Will. And the more times they do those things and the more of them they do, the more likely they are to leave a legacy. Anything that can remove an obstacle to further support is immensely valuable. And thank-you letters contribute to that success.

If the thanks is for a first gift, then it must include a welcome, with further information about the impact the donor is having with their gift to the charity's work. It could include a key element – a questionnaire. A large proportion of new supporters will fill it in and you will learn valuable information about their connection with your cause. As mentioned earlier, research builds 'active support'.

I suspect many readers are skipping this bit because they already send thank-you letters. Well done. But let me challenge you even if you are being impossibly smug.

Imagine I've just sent you a donation, say £50. Of course, you'll write to thank me. What words will you write after the bit that starts 'Dear Stephen'?

I'm sure many will be thinking: 'Dear Stephen, thank you for your kind gift of £50 which arrived today.' How **dull** is that? How boring that you should use the same words that nearly every fundraiser in nearly every charity throughout the world uses in their standard thank-you letter. What you are doing is reverting to your six-year-old self. You were taught to write this way by your mother when she demanded that you write to Granny to thank her for your Christmas present.

I have just shown you, if you care to admit it, how little you think of me the donor, and how readily you opt for unconsidered ideas and simple charity administrative processes. That's why donors feel un-appreciated, un-loved. Tell me you will never start another thank-you letter with such a dull opening line. And don't be pompous and write rubbish like this: 'On behalf of the Chairman, the board of trustees and the Chief Executive, I write to thank you for your kind gift of £50'. It is laughable, but thousands of charities write this way. It is **so** dull.

Actually it's more than that, it's madness. John Grain, an excellent fundraiser and consultant in the UK, carried out important research in 2010 for a series of thank-you letter workshops he was running. It showed that the thank-you letter was one of the most important communications a donor receives. Seven out of 10 people, when interviewed, said they had a better recall of the thank-you letter than the original appeal. And seven out of 10 people rated their thank-you letter as 'ordinary/predictable'. Yet it is so easy to make it personal and warm, or even kind and loving.

Stephen's rant 5

One more thing before I leave a subject that I hope is now accepted practice – all donations should receive thanks. In research groups, people will say that 'of course' they don't want precious funds wasted on thank-you letters. Don't believe them. The fundamental problem with research is that it is reason-based, logic-based. Most people's drive to support charities is emotion-based – logic doesn't come into it. And 'thanks' warms people emotionally, reminding them of that moment of satisfaction when they sent off their donation a few days earlier.

4.3 Invite them to join

To join what? The 'what' is not the important bit. Let's for a minute call it the Chief Executive's Club but promise never to use such a boring name!

What is it that differentiates a Major Donor from a Minor Donor? There are lots of things. Major Donors make gifts that have several noughts at the end of the number, they are allowed to earmark that money, the CEO is available whenever required and the donor is made to feel very special, significantly influential. One other factor differentiates a Major from a Minor Donor – the former is rich and the latter is not. In practice, it's likely the Minor Donor is actually making a bigger gift than the Major Donor, if viewed as a proportion of their available income.

So why can't Minor Donors enjoy some of the same interest from the CEO and other key figures in the charity? I don't mean after their first gift of £10, nor even after their second gift. But a third gift or third form of support indicates very significant commitment. And certainly, I would include anyone giving a monthly donation through their bank for more than say 15 or 18 months.

One reason a Minor Donor can't expect the same attention from the CEO as a Major Donor is clear; there are too many of them. But many of these Minor Donors have the potential to leave a legacy to the charity that will make the gifts of the rich pale into insignificance. And it is clear, the more a donor is involved with a charity, the more likely it is that they will leave a gift in their Will.

Not many CEOs think long-term about legacy income; most will have long-since retired when those promised gifts come through. And sadly, in the UK, where charities have benefited from legacy income for many years, some chief executives believe legacy income is their right and that it will continue to pour in like it always has. It won't, but more on that in Chapter 10.

Practical tips 4

So how should a fundraiser honour the ongoing commitment of a Minor Donor? I believe they need to be invited to a closer intimacy. Some will accept the invitation; most will not, but will feel warmed that they have been invited.

These people could receive a personal letter saying something like: 'Dear Mr. Pidgeon, the Chief Executive has suggested I write to you to ask if you would like to join his group of special supporters'. And the letter would go on to outline a relationship based entirely on occasional email correspondence – special briefings, news that is particularly pleasing, possible invitations to events, a greeting at Christmas and so on. What the letter is offering is a degree of 'specialness', a closeness to the organisation or just plain 'love'. And to accept the invitation, the supporter needs only to provide their email address.

Crude monthly emails are completely inappropriate. Correspondence should be occasional, no more than three or four times a year, with regular invitations to unsubscribe if required. It needs to be close and personal. The CEO is writing to a true friend of the charity. Of course, the correspondence does not actually come from the CEO. Let the CEO know it's happening, but this is a fundraising device run by fundraisers as part of a stewardship programme.

There is one more practical idea that would show a Minor Donor, so simply, how important their support is to the charity. It's very easy to do – every fundraiser looking after Minor Donors should implement this programme. Imagine your own reaction if, five years after you started your support of a charity, you received a short note, out of the blue, from the Chief Executive. 'Dear Mr. Pidgeon', it might say to me, 'I've noticed from our records that it was five years ago today that we received your first kind donation. I hope I've got the date right; I simply wanted to say how much we appreciate your support....'

I'd be blown away; I think most people would. And that's because charities normally behave like faceless monoliths. They do a great job, we send them money, they write to us in formal marketing-speak, but nobody **ever** gets personal. If the Chief Executive writes to me on the fifth anniversary of my support; that's really special.

And why stick to the fifth anniversary, what about the tenth or twentieth? Most charities will groan and say their records are not accurate. That may be true, but you could at least start with five years. And, once you've set it up, you don't actually have to do anything. The computer can produce the letter. Just stick it on the CEO's desk for their personal signature, and get it in the post. Do it every day!

4.4 Understand the importance of multi-channel communication

In 2012, Target Analytics, a Blackbaud company, issued figures[6] that have begun to influence serious fundraisers, though their significance is yet to dawn on many. Blackbaud regularly produces statistics on fundraising throughout the world that should be a wake-up call to naïve fundraisers still predicting the demise of offline fundraising techniques in favour of online ones in the next few years.

The figures show that where newly-acquired online donors use other channels to support the charity and become 'multi-channel' donors, their retention and long-term value goes up. Their individual gift value actually goes down but the additional frequency of giving more than compensates for it.

Happily, there is logic to the results. Supporters who follow their favourite charity through a number of media are likely to be more engaged. This report also shows that, of those recruited in 2009 through online channels, 32% had given in 2010 through direct mail, while 60% had stuck to online giving only.

The balance of 8% used other offline channels such as telephone. These simple results blow away the theory that if your donor is recruited online you should only ever talk to them online. It always was nonsense, a figment of the over-fertile imaginations of online fundraisers, anxious to take over the world!

Converting online-recruited people to using other channels appears to be relatively easy, but the opposite is more difficult. Of those recruited in 2009 through direct mail, only 3% were using online channels in 2010 (with 7% using other offline channels). Yet, given that people who give both online and through other channels are more

6 Blackbaud (2011) '2011 donor Centrics Internet and Multichannel Giving Benchmarking Report'. www.blackbaud.co.uk/targetananalytics/multi-channel-report

loyal than those who only give online, there is a clear challenge for fundraisers to encourage direct mail users to explore other channels as well.

Practical tips 5

In each medium used, the message and the images must match, though of course, each medium has different strengths that need to be exploited.

Direct mail supporters, mostly older people, use their computers all the time. They keep in touch with the grandchildren that way, watch the stock market, and use the Internet as a source of information. But it's not enough to dump an appeal on the website without building into it the elements that make that medium particularly influential. And access needs to be simple. For example, providing a short URL in a letter allows them direct access into your website to see more material to support your appeal.

And why not use personalised URL's – www.charityname.org/stephenpidgeon187, for instance? This way, a fundraiser can move a supporter from a mailed appeal to online where they can view rich media personalised to them. It can refer to previous donations or previous interests. It's no more difficult to organise than an old-fashioned mail merge, though probably it needs to be kept out of the hands of the technical staff within the charity. My old company frequently sends out mailings to several million households at a time, and each letter offers a unique personalised URL. In this way, the supporter can choose to respond offline or online. Not every supporter will use these personalised URLs; take-up will be slow at the beginning. But this is new in the charity sector and people will learn these different ways of accessing exciting information.

This is again something very simple to do. I do not understand why charities aren't using it, particularly overseas development charities. If the appeal is about something a thousand miles away from where I am, why can't the charity give me a URL that takes me onto Google Earth so I can physically see the area that the appeal is talking about? It wouldn't be difficult to show me different aspects of the project and I could click onto each bit to receive more detailed reviews, pictures, video and explanations.

And if I contribute to the building of a healthcare centre, for instance, or a school, a webcam could be set up to show me **my** centre. I could watch the thing being built, see it rise from the earth. This is **my** centre, my donation has contributed to it. Throughout the building process, I could receive updates on progress or otherwise. And finally, when it's finished, I could watch the opening ceremony. All this is possible; technologically, all this is easy. Only a small percentage of supporters will take up these interactive opportunities. But these few people, if treated well by the charity, could leave huge sums in legacies when they die. They have been engaged; they will feel loved. And they will reward you many times over.

5 Better stewardship

5.1 Let your donors choose how often they hear from you

Until just a few years ago, only one charity in the UK routinely offered its supporters the opportunity to choose how often they wanted to hear from it. It was Botton Village, now called The Camphill Family. It was doing great stewardship 20 years ago and has thrived throughout that time. A wonderful charity, it sends me a magazine three times a year telling me of progress in its communities. It's like a soap-opera – really lovely stuff and I feel treated like one of the family.

Offering your supporters some measure of control over how often you contact them honours their support and is increasingly valued in a society where people feel bombarded with information. Very few will opt out all together and if they do, then you would have been unlikely to get further support from them anyway. Some will ask only for an annual appeal – that's good, you save on costs and, when you write with that one appeal, you can remind them of their request with a strong ask. The response rates to this single appeal will be impressive.

The current thinking on when you should make the offer to tailor your contact with supporters to their wishes – and there are several charities starting to do this now – is that you must not do it too early, and certainly not after the first gift. After all, how will the new supporter know the pleasures of the stewardship programme that await them? You must test it, of course, but I would ask a new supporter after nine to 12 months, when they have experienced one or two appeals, a newsletter or two, maybe a prize draw mailing and whatever else you'd like them to respond to. Just at the point when they are wondering if they were wise to support your charity, you offer the option of being able to relax in their relationship with you. They resume control and that is a good feeling for them.

In compiling the options you offer them, you can influence their choice. You should try to make sure you are still able to send occasional and interesting newsletters, for instance, and, at the right moment, ask for an emergency donation or a gift in their Will. But you should always ask their forgiveness, lest they feel you are breaking your part of the arrangement.

5.2 Let them select what they support

There are all sorts of controversies in giving supporters choice. For years fundraisers have been browbeaten by finance colleagues to raise money that is not earmarked, so the charity can spend it as it chooses. It's time to hit back because supporters are increasingly interested in knowing exactly what their money is used for. It's not surprising. Major Donor fundraisers wouldn't dream of telling rich people their large gift will be spent where their Finance Director chooses. The same applies to people with less money but equal, if not more, passion for your cause.

UK charities are taking significant steps to allow supporters to choose, and they are to be congratulated. Cancer Research UK launched its MyProjects site (www.myprojects.cancerresearchuk.org) with the beguiling proposition: 'Choose the cancer you want to beat'. Brilliant. I've been hurt by cancer, as so many of us have, so I am angry and want to **beat** it, but I want to beat the specific cancer that took my loved-one, not just cancer in general. I want to stop it hurting others like it hurt me. And this site allows me to do that, which is immensely satisfying. I can choose which project I want my money to go to.

Another, taking its cue from the wonderful Kiva site that allows people to make micro-loans to entrepreneurs across the globe (www.kiva.org), is from Care UK – www.lendwithcare.org. It's a great title and much in the Kiva spirit. I can chose which projects I want my money to go to and what's even more interesting is that I am not making a gift, I'm making a loan. So one day my money will be returned.

In both these cases, the first step was to ignore the constraints of a generation of unimaginative charity finance directors and to allow the earmarking of donations by ordinary supporters. Financial directors need to get used to this. It's going to happen more and more often as Minor Donors become more vocal, demanding to know exactly what their money will achieve.

■ *Stephen's rant 6*

Now, the issue is clear – the money must go to whatever the donor was told it would go to. This is only right and if nothing else, the UK Institute of Fundraising Code of Practice requires it. But why can't financial people be more flexible? Many only ascribe to a project the direct costs of running that project. Why? No commercial company would do that. In the charitable world, no work would get done unless there were non-project costs – a fundraiser or two, part of an accounts staff member, a receptionist, heating, lighting and everything else. Why not allocate fixed costs right across the project budget?

When I ran my commercial agency, I saw multiple versions of the parent company's accounts, all accurate, all prepared under the law but drawn up for different functions. Why can't financial staff in charities think this way? They have to change, because Minor Donors now want a measure of control over where their money is being spent, not just Major Donors. And why shouldn't they?

To give financial staff their due, every time I have asked a finance director to be more flexible in their demands for un-earmarked funds, they have always been helpful. Fundraisers must tackle the issue and sort it out.

5.3 Offer a money-back guarantee

Why not? How impressive would it be as a supporter to be told that, if you were ever concerned that your gift was not being used wisely, you could have it back, no questions asked? There would have to be some time limit on the offer, of course, perhaps six months.

The guarantee was the idea of the innovative John Grain when he was at Habitat for Humanity in the UK. Now, my clear-thinking client in Dublin, Irish Red Cross, uses it routinely in every appeal. It is just part of the conditions of support. Apart from one or two nuisance demands when the offer was first made (at the time, Irish Red Cross were going through some challenges), no-one has ever asked for their donation back.

Just think what would happen if a supporter phoned up in a rage asking for their money back because of some concern they had about your charity? You'd get your Director of Fundraising to speak to them, hear them out, answer their queries… and either give their money back or send them away a 'supporter for life'.

5.4 Choose where to invest your energies

Stewardship can be expensive, though I believe passionately that good stewardship will lead to a transformation in the charity's finances as delighted supporters change their Wills in your favour. But until I can prove that, restricting your efforts to your more valuable supporters will at least get you started.

Invest in these valuable supporters. Split your supporter file (all of it) into 10 deciles (10% segments) by net value. In other words, look at what each supporter has given you and take away the cost of the appeals, newsletters, prize draws and everything else you've sent them in their time with you.

It's a straightforward analysis, though it's probably better to make it slightly more complicated by giving extra weight to those who have been supporting you for only a short time. But keep it as simple as possible. Then invest a lot of energy (and money!) in the segments that give the most, decreasing the investment as the segments get less valuable. Don't throw out those with low or negative value; simply reduce contact with them to maintenance levels. These segments will still yield legacies at some point in the future.

Practical tips 6

This sort of analysis is all part of stewardship. It will also throw up other key patterns for you. For example:

– In health charities it is highly likely that some supporters will give once per year at a particular time, no doubt a time of great significance to them. Your contact programme for those supporters should reflect that seasonality

– Many supporters show a preference for one or two areas of your charity's work over others. Again, the moment you've spotted the pattern, their personal programme should reflect this

– People respond to different styles of appeal. I remember working with an animal charity and sending out mailings that were alternately cutsie and viciously graphic. It would have been astonishing if the same donors had responded to both and if you talked to them, those liking the cutsie appeals said they simply threw the 'horrid ones' in the bin unopened. They couldn't cope with the graphic images and why should they? But the charity continued to send them anyway. Why? Because no-one could be bothered to do the simple analysis and reflect the donor's wishes. That was unacceptable then and it is now plain stupid, and counter to any thought of good stewardship. It's also a waste of money.

5.5 Invite your donors to see the impact of their gifts

I support many charities and a few of them regularly invite me to attend a local briefing on their work and the impact of my gifts. Brilliant. For example, one invitation from Oxfam was to join a group of other supporters in a pub in my local town of Cheltenham. I couldn't go, but I was pleased to have been asked. Oxfam also routinely invites me to join a webinar, where I can ask questions about its work or strategy. And, because its fundraisers are smart, they write to me afterwards inviting me to view the questions the webinar dealt with and the replies given. I don't know how many people join these events, but, as a supporter, I appreciate being asked. And my confidence in the charity's work increases because it is prepared to be open to challenge and criticism.

Charities should take every opportunity to invite their supporters to local briefings, openings of new facilities, open days and so on. As a supporter, it's good to be asked. But there are other strong benefits.

I was once at a Donor Day in a care centre due to be opened next day. The builders were still all over the place and staff members were frantic. About 30 donors turned up (out of some 3,000 invited – remember, always invite them to bring a friend) to see the wonderful facility that their donations had provided. They were a merry bunch, knowledgeable, articulate, brimming with questions, and the staff members detailed to look after them were soon won over. Most of the donors were women in their seventies. The staff suddenly realised who was paying their salaries; these donors were. Never again did the fundraisers lack for stories for their appeals.

5.6 What happens if they stop their monthly gift?

The short answer with many charities worldwide is 'nothing'. Sometimes, after a few weeks, the monthly donor is sent an administrative letter. Nowadays, that's not good enough.

In the UK, because we were the first to push the idea of a monthly gift, paid automatically through the bank, we made a mistake that we now struggle to change. We started asking for £2 per month. In practice, that £2 per month is upgraded through phone calls to higher sums over the years, but essentially we started by asking far too little. Other countries, learning from our mistakes perhaps, have done well to achieve larger monthly gifts.

If I pay a charity £2 a month and decide I don't want to do it any more, cancelling it is easy – a few minutes online and payment is stopped. If the charity doesn't come back to me within a very short time then my feeling that it was never very valuable to the charity in the first place, is compounded.

Charities must follow up cancelled automatic payments as soon as possible and certainly no later than one month's payment cycle. But what do you say when you call? Here are two alternatives, both designed to make the monthly donor feel 'reasonable' after the guilt of cancelling their payment.

The first would be to offer a 'payment holiday'. You agree with the donor that the cancellation is actually temporary and a phone call to consider re-instating it is arranged for three or four months' time.

If the monthly payment is more substantial, say £20 per month, then the donor can be offered a reduced payment for an agreed period. Donors' finances fluctuate; what you don't want to vary is their commitment to the wonderful work of your charity. You should bend over backwards to reassure the donor that their ongoing support is essential, even if it is not going to be backed with their financial support for a few months.

5.7 Make your approach relevant to the donor

It's March and you are about to send out your Spring appeal. The chances are, the whole active database will get the same appeal. Smarter fundraisers will have a variable opening paragraph, which relies on some aspect of the relationship between the donor and your charity. That's good. And many will ask for gifts that relate to values received in the past. That's good too.

But it's not nearly enough in today's information-led age. At the very least, you should ensure that people giving in different value bands get different styles of appeal. People giving low-value gifts need a very simple ask, possibly incentivised with name and address labels or other small premium. It should be a simple story, a picture or two, nothing more.

At the other end of the spectrum, high-value people require a lot of detailed information about the project. The higher the value of the gift you are asking for, the more information you need to provide – charts, maps, plans, reports from the field. These people demand to know in detail why their money is needed and what will be achieved if they give it.

And in the middle, supporters giving anything between say, £20 and £200, need a well argued case, good story line, some pictures and no premiums.

The topic of the appeal can be common to all value groups; it is the style of the appeal that must vary. If you have a massive database, then every appeal will have several versions, appeals that look and feel completely different, though the topic is the same. In the UK, that star of Minor Donor fundraising, Save the Children, does this routinely.

If you have a smaller database, varying each appeal is just impractical, which is why, in most charities, the same appeal goes out to everyone. So, very few of your supporters actually get what they need. Start to differentiate which of your supporters gets what type of pack. Ensure that at least once or twice per year, a donor who has given £250 gets an appeal full of detailed information. And don't waste your money sending that appeal to a donor who has only ever given £5. Equally, don't anger donors who are happy to give sizeable donations, because they directly connect their gift with the impact you tell them it will have, by sending them tacky appeals full of premiums, prize draws and other incentives. If they respond to them, their lifetime value will go **down**. You will teach them to look for an incentive before they make their gift.

▬▬ *Stephen's rant 7*

All this adds up to one key principle; we must stop asking our supporters so often, with inappropriate appeals. Fundraisers' ability to destroy a relationship with their supporters never ceases to amaze me. The obvious stupidity is over-mailing. In the past, we did it because it was profitable. If you take legacy income into account and think long term, then it is catastrophically unprofitable. It ruins relationships because your supporters see that you are not treating them as valued individual contributors to your cause. They feel you are abusing them.

And I've seen some truly ignorant appeals: renewal letters demanding to know why the supporter hasn't given a donation recently; appeal letters so full of politically correct pompous jargon that they are frankly patronising; upgrade letters expressed in terms of some sleazy 'deal' – 'If you (supporter) increase your monthly gift to us (charity) then we'll…..' and the 'deal' is laid out, usually in administrative terms designed to make the charity's life easier. Supporters see through these shabby requests and, though a few give more, others will stop their support all together.

If a donor hasn't made a donation, despite three or four of the very best appeals (which include the style and topic of the appeal that first recruited them), then stop mailing them appeals. Do something else to interest them. Phone them, invite them to something, send them a handwritten note. Do something that breaks the mould of boring appeal letters. They might then feel they are important to you.

5.8 Is all this stewardship stuff worth it?

So far, you've seen loads of simple ideas to improve the stewardship of your Minor Donors, and to do it cost-effectively. All have the single purpose of improving the experience your supporters have of your charity. And there are dozens of other ideas. All that is required is a different attitude to supporters, and a longer-term view of their immense potential value. Stewardship requires fundraisers to provide their supporters with great emotional experiences. And, in most charities I know, that will only be achieved through a fundamental change of attitude towards supporters. Long-term thinking must prevail, overcoming demands for short-term income.

The key is to look for ways to communicate with your supporters or meet them as often as you can, commensurate with their value.

For example, there is currently an explosion of interest in social media and the opportunities it offers charities. These are wonderfully numerous, and one day charities will raise serious amounts of money by these means. For me, the really exciting thing is the commitment by fundraisers that, when working through social media, the individual is important and the fundraiser's job is two-fold – to spot what turns them on and provide the right stimulus to generate new interest. What a pity such energy and concentration on individual supporters through social media is not applied equally to donors supporting through direct mail – if it were, the impact on the charity's finances would be transforming.

I have never seen a lifetime value analysis that includes legacy gifts. Most pundits see it as distasteful, though I rather like the idea of a lifetime and a death-time value! Legacy marketing only started seriously in the UK in 1986 when WWF asked its members, donors and the general public for pledges, and there are still relatively few charities that can trace a majority of legacy gifts back to the supporters on their database. Adding it into a lifetime value calculation gets a bit tricky but is not impossible. And I believe there is an indisputable logic that if the loyalty and commitment of a particular supporter is truly matched by the faithfulness of the charity to provide consistently positive, satisfying experiences, then the lifetime value will rise, and the lifetime plus death-time value will go through the roof.

In the next chapter I will explore another key factor in providing great supporter experiences – delivering consistent fundraising messages. Marketing folk will immediately assume the next chapter is about branding but it's not. I'm leaving my scathing comments on issues to do with charity brands for later.

6 Finding your fundraising proposition

6.1 Answering the 'killer question'

Supporters are often baffled by the inconsistency in the messages that come out of their favourite charity. Because many different fundraisers speak to supporters, not to mention communications people and other colleagues, most charities are neither clear nor consistent about what will be achieved if the supporter makes a donation.

What is needed is a simple fundraising proposition – variably called the 'elevator pitch', 'case for support' and many other names. Your fundraising proposition answers the killer question: 'Why should I give your charity £200 now'? My arrogant view is that if you can't answer the question, then you should get out of fundraising. Doubtless many readers are confident of their position.

I choose £200 – that's my figure, personal to me and yours might be different. But the point is the same. If I was moved by a particular need and felt I could do something about it, then I could give £200, but that's quite a lot and I'd have to think about it. The argument for it would have to be persuasive.

Now, let me challenge your confidence. Try writing your answer down. When you've got some words on paper, the next challenge is to show them to a fundraising colleague in your charity. In most cases, your version and your colleague's will differ, sometimes by a lot. And if you really want a laugh, ask your service provision or communications staff to do the same exercise. Likely as not, they won't have a clue!

Yet the answer to the question is at the heart of a fundraiser's work. Actually, it's at the heart of the work of everybody in a charity, because most charities have to ask for money. Asking for money is the one thing that is common to charities – that's an interesting thought, given the poor status of fundraising in many charities!

Most people in charities will answer the question with a list of activities: 'We help lonely old people by providing pop-in centres, free meals and transport' or 'We rescue animals that have suffered and we do that by….'. But as I said at the beginning of Chapter 4; nobody is interested in what you or your charity **does** (except perhaps, you and your colleagues). People are only interested in what your charity **achieves** when you do it – people helped, dogs saved, environment protected and so on.

So no-one is interested in paying for 'centres' or 'meals' or 'transport' or 'rescue services'. But they will be really pleased to help pay for the smiles and the new confidence that comes from a weekly gathering where local older people can be picked up to meet their friends and benefit from a little pampering. They will be sad at the loneliness that prompted the need for that pop-in centre, but warm to the enjoyment that their donation has made possible.

This is basic stuff. It's the equivalent of a sales trainer in a commercial environment teaching people to sell the **benefits** of a product (the change the product will make to the customer's life), rather than its **features** – what it does, how it works and so on.

But here is the crunch, and I've heard the comment hundreds of times. 'Our charity does so many things for so many people, how can you express that in one or two sentences?' The answer is 'you have to'.

Did the UK children's charity, NSPCC, cut its range of services or reduce the numbers of children helped when it declared that 'Cruelty to children must stop. Full stop!' Of course not, but look at its staggering fundraising success since it was able to answer the killer question with: 'Your support will help us to stop cruelty to children. Full stop.' Supporters don't want to know the detail of how it goes about doing that; they just want to know that cruelty is being stopped.

Another UK charity, Sue Ryder Care, began to describe its work as 'caring for people who are seriously ill'. The details of its clients' terminal or neurological conditions were irrelevant to the more important issue that support is needed for people who are seriously ill.

6.2 How do you find your fundraising proposition?

The fundraising proposition does not lie in a charity's vision statement, mission statement and all the other products of old-fashioned brand reviews. There is nothing wrong with these things, but they are designed for internal use and have to be translated before they are relevant to supporters. The job of the fundraising proposition is to motivate supporters.

My old agency (Tangible) devised and copyrighted a model to help fundraisers break down the key elements of a charity's mission in ways that will motivate supporters. In essence, the model takes on the big 'hard to answer' question – 'Why should I give you £200?' – and asks four questions instead, which are easier to answer. We call it the Four Pillars Exercise©. Copyrighting means you can use the model but if you show it in public, you must acknowledge its source. The model assumes the fundraising proposition rests on at least three of four possible pillars, which we describe as Vision, Enemy, Hero and Recipient.

The **Vision** describes the charity's ultimate goal, the pinnacle of success that means the charity has no more work to do. The agency never worked with the RNLI (the UK's wonderful volunteer lifeboat service) but using it as an example, its ultimate Vision would be 'no more deaths at sea'. If there were no more deaths at sea, the RNLI wouldn't need to exist. In discussions, there will always be someone who trots out the corporate vision. I have never known it to be anything but irrelevant, written only for internal use. The Vision pillar in this model should describe the ultimate success that would allow the charity to pack up and go home, with the job finished. It is the nature of this Vision that it will never be achieved.

The **Enemy**, the second pillar, is simple – what evil, what misfortune or injustice, prevents the Vision from being achieved? In the RNLI example, the Enemy is the sea. It's cold, it's wet and it's frequently angry. So, while it exists, we will always need the RNLI to save us from it. The Enemy is usually a strong pillar, a gift to fundraisers because having a 'baddie' to defeat makes for a simple call to action. This is not in the case for the RNLI because there's not much a donor can do about the sea, it will always be there!

The third pillar is the **Hero**. The Hero is a principle, a team, a person that is fighting the Enemy to achieve the Vision. For the RNLI, it's the heroic members of the lifeboat crew, and the fact that they are all volunteers is a gift for writers working on RNLI appeals. They are not even paid to be brave – fantastic! I've run this exercise for hundreds of clients across the world, mostly charities but increasingly for theatres, museums and other organisations wanting to know what they can say that will move people to make a donation. In practically all of these discussions, at some point someone will say, 'well, the Hero is the donor'. In this model, the Hero is usually the person, the thing that my donation pays for to fight the Enemy. The donor cannot therefore feature.

And the last pillar, the **Recipient**, is the person, people or thing that benefits from that fight. In the case of the RNLI, many of the Recipients are actually pretty foolish. The Recipient is the yachtsman who gets into trouble because he hasn't prepared well enough for his journey, or the youngsters climbing on the rocks who forget that the incoming tide will cut them off from the shore.

The RNLI advertisement that for 20 years has pulled in new support has a picture of a volunteer crewman in lifeboat kit. The piercing eyes of the bearded lifeboatman (the **Hero**) who fights the great sea storms around our island (the **Enemy**) demand support, and that's enough for anyone who is British. The lifeboatman is always bearded and always a man. I'm not being sexist; tests with pictures of women and clean-shaven men show these images are less effective. British folk like our lifeboatmen rugged! Meanwhile, Britishness and the RNLI in this context are synonymous and imply the **Vision**. No mention is made of the **Recipient**. They just don't go there because it's unnecessarily complicated.

Out of the Four Pillars Exercise© will come a clear statement that answers the killer question 'Why should I give you £200 now?'. Not every message from the charity needs to contain the statement, indeed, it may never be used. The statement describes the feeling supporters are left with whenever they see your literature, visit your website, think about your work or talk to your colleagues; which is why it's so important to involve colleagues in the discussions.

Supporters will understand the good that will be achieved when they donate their money or their time. And that's a step worth fighting for. If your charity gets its fundraising proposition right and delivers it consistently, its fundraising will be transformed.

6.3 From pillars to proposition – some examples

Kind colleagues and friends have agreed to the use of these examples; my grateful thanks to them.

Let me start with Sue Ryder Care, which provides wonderful neurological and palliative care through its care centres in the UK. Finding words that described what care it offers (when it is so diverse) and to whom (other people who I don't know much about) was a considerable challenge. Staff found their own way of describing their work, usually based on their own local care centre. This was little help to fundraisers who wanted a simple, unifying message to motivate supporters to give to the charity as a whole.

The breakthrough in discussions came when all the complex medical conditions affecting those receiving the care were boiled down to the simple description of the charity's Vision pillar: 'To help every seriously ill person to have the best quality of life'. Instantly, complex neurological conditions like Multiple Sclerosis, Alzheimers, Muscular Dystrophy and Motor Neurone Disease, plus the need for palliative pain relief in the period before death, were reduced to a few words that a supporter would understand – 'seriously ill' with the possibility offered of 'the best quality of life'.

For those delivering the care, it was an unwelcome simplification; for fundraisers it was a big step to easier fundraising. Remember, supporters are not interested in the detail of what the charity does; it is irrelevant. They want to know what happens when that work is done well.

The Enemy pillar was again, unhelpful. The Enemy was essentially the lack of enough good care available in the UK's National Health Service and it's too difficult to hang a fundraising ask on a pillar like that. In essence, you would be asking the donor to replace money that Government should provide and, emotionally, that's just too hard to accept.

The Hero pillar was easy – the passionate and expert care staff – but how were we to describe the wide range of Recipients? We reduced it to three words – 'someone I love'. That allows for 'connection', it makes any ask relevant to 'me'. Any one of us might, at some stage, need Sue Ryder Care's wonderful service.

So the four pillars looked like this:

Vision	Enemy	Hero	Recipient
To help every seriously ill person to have the best quality of life	The limited availability of the best quality care	Passionate and expert carers	Someone I love

This led to the fundraising proposition: 'When someone you love is seriously ill, our passionate, expert carers will help them enjoy the best life they can in the time they have.'

What that single sentence does is leave the donor with a clear feeling about the difference they make if they give a donation. Effectively, they will be donating 'best life' to a 'seriously ill person' 'in the time they have'. Again, let me confirm that the actual words are not essential. What is required for a consistent and emotional message is the feeling contained in the words. Ask yourself the question: 'When a supporter reads the appeal I've just written (or the press release or even the service leaflet), will they get the feeling described in the proposition above?' If they do, then the proposition is being delivered. If they don't, start again!

For my second example I'm taking you to Norway. City Mission operates in every city looking after people living on the street. Its work is wonderful, supporting homeless people completely without judgement.

Vision	Enemy	Hero	Recipient
Everybody in my city living their life with dignity	Life's hardship that is sometimes too hard to carry	City Mission people who help them carry their load	The person fighting, with courage, to turn their life around

And out of the four pillars comes this answer to the question: 'Why should I give you Kr2,000?': 'When someone's life has gone past breaking point, your Kr2,000 will ensure that someone from City Mission, who can see a way out, will help them start to live the life they would have chosen.'

Effectively, my gift helps one person to turn their life around. I feel good with that thought. I'm not particularly interested in how City Mission does it, but I do want to know that my support has made it possible. That gives me real satisfaction – which is why giving feedback to supporters on the impact of their donations is so important.

My third example is a mid-sized UK charity called Elizabeth Finn Care (EFC). It used to be called The Distressed Gentlefolk Aid Association, a name which perfectly described its client profile, but in ways so old-fashioned that a change of name was essential. EFC's mistake, some 10 years ago, was renaming the organisation after its founder, an obscure Victorian woman unknown to any but those very close to the charity's work. Under its new name, EFC described its clientele as 'professional people', which helped very little. At one point, it compiled a list of the 'professions' whose members it would support, and at the top of the list was accountants! It was of little practical help and hopeless for fundraising.

So we were not only grappling with the need for a fundraising proposition, but with a client group it was virtually impossible to describe. Again the Four Pillars Exercise© came into its own. The discussion was greatly enhanced by contributions from some of those who distributed the money and others who had benefited from it.

The four pillars came out like this:

Vision	Enemy	Hero	Recipient
Returning a measure of financial independence	The hand that life deals	The understanding that professional people sometimes need help too	People, like you and me, now forced to live on life's financial edge

Reasonable financial independence was the Vision, 'fate' was the Enemy and this time the Hero was simply a recognition that even people who have been independent and self-sufficient all their lives can end up struggling through no fault of their own. The Recipients could then be described as 'just like you or me'.

The fundraising proposition still contained the dreaded 'P-word' (professional) but as discussed, a fundraising proposition is an internal document and its job is to describe a feeling. It went like this: 'Your gift of £200 means we can give professionals, just like you or me, who have fallen on hard times, a degree of financial independence and the special help they need'.

So, how does this appear when translated into an appeal or an advertisement? This is the copy from an ad in Autumn 2009 asking for legacy gifts. Notice how the concept of 'professionals, just like you' is interpreted without any need for a detailed explanation of EFC's client group.

Under a picture of a white-haired woman in her mid-seventies, the headline read: 'She's never asked for help. So we're doing it for her.' The copy read: 'Mary is one of our country's many proud, hard-working people. Good people who've always given more to society than they've taken from it. But today Mary, a former nurse, is really struggling. Illness meant she had to give up her part-time job. Her husband's funeral took her savings. Now rising food and fuel bills are taking her pension and her dignity. A victim of awful circumstance, someone who's been kind all her life now needs our kindness.'

The ad goes on to explain how a gift in your Will can help people like Mary. There is a striking final sentence: 'Because, when life gets too tough, good people should stick together and look out for one another.' It's a sentiment that many elderly people in the UK would support fully.

You are probably thinking what ghastly schmaltzy stuff this is. I couldn't care less, the ad is not aimed at you. It's aimed at a particular group of elderly British women who would get to the end of it and think: 'That poor woman is just like me'. They are the people the charity is targeting with its legacy ask. It was a very successful advertisement for a traditional charity doing wonderful work.

Practical tips 7

The Four Pillars Exercise© is a great discipline but needs skilled hands. Here are some tips on how to get it right:

- Invite your senior fundraisers, of course, but also your communications colleagues. They are often good at articulating each of the pillars but their involvement in the expression of the charity's proposition means they also begin to understand key fundraising principles such as 'nobody is interested in what your charity does'. Campaigners too should be invited; it is a great way to build bridges with a key group of colleagues. And, because they are the ones that distribute the money you raise and therefore see its impact, you'll find the inclusion of one or two service delivery colleagues is an asset

- Get someone to chair the discussion who is experienced enough to control people who don't listen, like the senior person who trots out the corporate vision statement – they are probably one of the few who has ever read it. They need to be slapped down firmly but positively

- Depending on how good the Chair is, limit the group to no more than 15

- Get all your colleagues to write down their pillars one pillar at a time, at least for the first two or three, then write them on a board for all to see. Do all of that before any discussions start. The best articulation of a pillar often comes from unexpected sources

- If you find you are struggling with the Enemy, Hero or Recipient pillars, then it's probably because the Vision is not right. Everything goes back to the Vision pillar

- The words in the final proposition usually come directly from the four pillars. Putting the words together should again be done individually, with each member of the group working quietly. Get the different versions up on the board before letting discussions start on which best answers the question 'Why should I give you £200'?

- If the words in the final agreed proposition don't come out of the pillars, yet you are content that the proposition gives a clear statement of what a donation to your charity will achieve, then don't worry about it. The pillars are simply a means to an end; they have no merit in themselves.

Every fundraiser needs a fundraising proposition. Without it, they cannot answer my question 'Why should I give you £200 now'?

A limited number of fundraisers, however, need a change in their charity's brand. Yet, driven by vested interests, so many charities rush into a hugely expensive re-branding exercise with the odd notion that the greater the awareness a new brand will bring, the greater will be the transformation of their voluntary income. Far too often the decision to review the brand is made without even consulting the fundraisers. And these reviews are happening more and more, hence the next chapter with its tales of extraordinary success and abject failure.

7 All you need to know about charity brands

The unchallenged comparison with the commercial sector in matters of charity brands has been the source of vast sums of wasted money by charities in the UK. And at least some of the waste has resulted from fundraisers not being clear and focused on the value of re-branding. Fundraisers have allowed such exercises to go on around them without demanding answers to the simple question: 'Why *exactly* are we doing this'? Hence this chapter.

There are fundamental differences between non-profit and commercial brands. There are lots of similarities too and, in the last few years, most of the successful brand re-launches in the UK have been master-minded by agencies that also work in the commercial field. But these successes have been rooted in a deep understanding of the differences between commercial and charity brands. There are basically three.

7.1 Difference 1: Charities have no tangible product

Commercial companies sell products with tangible benefits to the purchaser, both physical and emotional. There is an exchange of value – payment on one side, benefit on the other. Charities don't do that, of course. A donor sends money and receives only private, deep, emotional satisfaction. That's why fundraisers must do much more to produce consistent and rewarding emotional experiences.

It's also why some donors question what might, to charity staff, appear to be irrelevant matters of detail such as the cost of administration or the CEO's salary.

A careful explanation would probably convince them this was money well spent. But we don't operate in the logical, 'careful explanation' business. The joy of our sector is that we deal with raw emotion, the sort of emotion that we can use to link supporters with both problems and solutions.

Commercial companies spend a lot of money on 'awareness advertising' to remind their customers of the link between payment and benefit. Some charities try to do it too, but fail lamentably – it makes supporters ask questions like: 'Why is this charity saying these things, what's the point?' and it confuses them. But more of that later.

7.2 Difference 2: You have few distinguishing values

Difference two is more complex and comes out of a paper by Professors Adrian Sargeant and John Ford in 2007[2]. Commercial brands fight to differentiate themselves. Charity brands actually benefit from being similar.

Sargeant and Ford argue that simply being a charity automatically implies beneficial values such as compassion, effectiveness, trust or honesty. All charities benefit from this and it grieved me in my role as Chairman of the Institute of Fundraising's Standards Committee when I used to hear, occasionally, of rogue charities exploiting supporters' innate beliefs that everything charitable was good. These unscrupulous charities were expert at turning such naivety into dubious profit.

Charity values are inherited by every charity. And within a charity sector (such as overseas development), all the charities in that sector inherit those values. So where are the opportunities to distinguish your charity's brand from others? They are pretty limited.

The Sargeant and Ford research shows they are confined to four key areas: what emotions the charity can create; the tone of its voice in the media; the nature of its service; and its ties with tradition. Every charity needs to have defined how it will exploit these four key areas.

7 Sargeant A. and Ford J. (Winter 2007) 'The Power of Brands'. Stanford Social Innovation Review. www.ssireview.org/articles/entry/the_power_of_brands

7.2.1 What emotions you can create

If you look at any of the UK charities that have been successful at recruiting new donors, every message is full of raw and rewarding emotion. Take Cancer Research UK with its sublime TV ad from 2011, showing people talking directly to camera and explaining how it feels to have cancer. In the course of the 60-second ad, up to 20 people speak and the stories are all so similar. It is the story of fighting cancer, and it finishes by implying it's not a battle that everyone will win.

Another example is the Smile Train mailshot showing pretty kids devastated by a hair lip and offering the donor the chance to change all that for one child. Or the message from Dog's Trust through the picture of a dog looking straight at you with big dark eyes – 'Will you give your love to me'? The list is endless and the genre, based almost exclusively on the use of eyes in pictures, is well established. How surprising then that so many charities ignore emotion, many specifically writing it out of the images and copy they use.

Stephen's rant 8

I grieve at fundraisers who ruin emotional copy. Faced with winning copy that links the donor emotionally with the beneficiary, fundraisers start wielding their red pen, often making changes in the name of political correctness. Working for a children's charity, we were told we couldn't describe the abusive mother of a teenage child as 'an alcoholic' – it was deemed a pejorative term. Our plea that it explained why this mother did such appalling things to her daughter, perhaps offering hope for the future, was denied. The amended mailshot didn't do very well. I wonder why!

A wonderful quote, often attributed to David Ogilvy, the legendary head of the Ogilvy and Mather (O&M) advertising agency, goes like this: 'The strongest desire is not love or hate…but the need to change someone else's copy.'

Junior fundraisers feel this acutely – they need to justify their existence – and sadly, it is most often junior fundraisers who are entrusted to read the first draft copy for a campaign. They generally have little experience in fundraising and are 50 years younger than the audience for which the copy has been written, but confident in their degree-level knowledge of English, they routinely apply two kisses of death. They change the short, journalistic style of writing to something more literate, and they take out the emotion. Their logic is that their boss, the Head of Individual Fundraising, would not want to see copy that was inelegant.

Now, the Head of Individual Fundraising is experienced, but is given copy that is OK but not good enough to show the Director of Fundraising. So, they change it some more, anticipating the Director's views on good copy. When the Director of Fundraising finally sees it, the copy is rubbish. 'Who wrote this'? enquires the Director and, in unison, the executive and the Head of Individual Fundraising say: 'The agency'!

Well, of course, the agency didn't write the stuff that was shown to the Director; its original copy had been ruined by people with no skill and little understanding.

*Now this doesn't happen every time or in every charity. But it happens a **lot**; I'd say it happens in the majority of cases. The position would be much improved if all fundraisers spent at least one day every three months (just 1% of their time) talking to real Minor Donors. Most never meet them.*

If you are a fundraiser looking at early-draft copy, you have only two jobs. You first have to check the facts are right, the brand is maintained and people are honoured. Secondly, you have to judge whether you think it will move your supporters. If it won't, then throw it back for re-writing. Explain exactly why you don't like it and what changes you want made. But leave your red pen alone; you are not a copywriter.

7.2.2 The tone of your charity's voice in the media

The second key area in which a charity can distinguish itself is its tone. Why are some media messages so clear and so predictable? It's because the tone is established and consistent. Literally, the tone has been created, then maintained. So the brand is strengthened. Charities in the UK like Christian Aid, NSPCC, Greenpeace, and in the US like Mothers against Drunk Drivers (MADD), Harvesters, or The Brady Campaign to Prevent Gun Violence have tough messages delivered in a forthright tone. The Royal British Legion speaks with the authoritative tone of over 90 years of wonderful work. Oxfam, Shelter and many others are always consistent in the way they express themselves – others are all over the place.

Take a line and stick to it. But don't, in any circumstances, let the line be established by people who have no responsibility for raising the money. Because most will float off into cloud-cuckoo-land and deliver messages in a tone that will never work for fundraising. And your job, and the charity's job, is first and foremost to raise money. Without money, a charity has no mission.

7.2.3 The nature of your service

Charities differ in the services they deliver. So the Royal National Institute for Blind People (RNIB) and Action for Blind People both do excellent work supporting people with sight problems. The way they do that is completely different and this is reflected in the way they express themselves. You can spot the difference in their nature simply in the look and feel of their mailings. RNIB is authoritative and influential but corporate. Action for Blind People tells stories, gives detail, solves problems. Indeed, so different, but so complementary are the two charities, that they are now merged administratively, though not for fundraising purposes.

7.2.4 Your ties to tradition

And finally, for some charities, traditions and origins are crucial for fundraising, particularly while we still have a donating generation whose collective memory stretches back to the early part of the 20th Century. On the supporter base of The Royal British Legion, for instance, there is a huge group of supporters who only ever respond to a request for a donation to celebrate an event in WWI or WWII. Why would they do that, in their hundreds of thousands, some 70 or 100 years later? The celebration of courage involved in these events is at the heart of the values that these supporters hold dear.

More modern charities have 'traditions' too; it's part of what distinguishes them from others. Crisis helps homeless people throughout the year but its 'tradition' is their work around Christmas.

7.3 Difference 3: You're not solely about making money

'Driver of Ideas' Joe Saxton of nfpSynergy has expressed his views on the difference between charity and commercial brands in a number of papers, for instance Polishing the Diamond[8]. Commercial companies sell goods or services to make a profit, so the whole organisation is focused on that activity. In charities, service provision can, and sadly, often does, operate as a completely separate entity from marketing or fundraising.

In commerce, the moment sales of Widget A decline, manufacturing is switched to Widget B. The decision is taken collectively as part of the corporate strategy. In charities, the services provided often bear little relationship to the consumer fundraising messages. The two operate in isolation. And, as Saxton points out, there is a further dilemma, for instance, with certain disadvantaged groups. Showing people who have, say, learning difficulties in a positive light, emphasising what they can do rather than what they can't leads members of the public to adopt a more positive attitude and life becomes easier all round. But need, difference and the inability to lead a 'normal' life is the stuff upon which fundraising thrives.

In many charities, fundraising is tolerated as a necessary evil. This attitude stems right from the top. Most boards of trustees are only interested in service provision; many chief executives find the black art of fundraising both impenetrable and vulgar. They love talking to those charming rich people who might give a major gift. But they simply have neither experience nor knowledge of dealing with Minor Donors on a massive database.

This is never more evident than in charities looking to re-brand. Who owns the brand?

8 Saxton J. (2002) 'Polishing the Diamond', nfpSynergy, London. www.nfpsynergy.net/polishing-diamond

Is it the service provision staff with their marketing mouthpiece, the communications department, or the fundraisers whose job it is to persuade people to give their financial or voluntary support?

In charities where this dilemma is debated and addressed, the resolution leads to greatly improved fundraising and expanding service provision. But in many cases it's not. You can spot charities where there is friction between fundraisers and service or communication staff, and it's a tragedy. Case studies become hard to find. Service staff take no part in fundraising events. Ignorant comments are made about supporters like 'we can't ask them again, they've just given', implying money always has to be dragged out of donors and they only ever give reluctantly. Fundraisers know that providing supporters with timely opportunities to give actually pleases them. **They wouldn't do it otherwise.**

7.4 What is the impact of these differences?

There are several implications and they all come to a head when a charity wants to re-brand. The first question to ask is: '**Why do we want to do it'?** The inevitable answer is: 'to build awareness' – because that's what a commercial company would say. Re-branding exercises are conducted at a very senior level, with the board of trustees and CEO always involved both because of the costs and the fact that it's a glamorous process that senior people like to dabble in. Everybody wants to have their say and most of these people, knowing nothing about such things, are happy with the notion that 'we should review our brand to build awareness'.

So the second and obvious question is: '**Why do you want to build awareness'?**

In the commercial world greater awareness is widely understood to lead to higher sales, though in most commercial sectors, even this mantra is now challenged. Yet no such link between awareness and income has ever been established in the charity world.

But let's answer that simple question. How about, we need to build awareness because:

- We'll get more supporters that way.
- More old people will die leaving us a legacy in their Will.
- We'll find more clients if more people are aware of what we do.
- The government will notice us more and that's important.
- People will support our campaign to change the law on….whatever it is!

All these are excellent reasons to 'build awareness'. But there are two difficulties with such an approach. No charity can **ever** spend enough money building its brand to the point where these five objectives can be achieved. It would require seven or eight figure budgets every year for three years to put even a small dent in the public's awareness.

The second problem is that there are many more effective strategies to achieve all of these five objectives. If you want more supporters, then ask the right audience for a donation using the right story and the right medium for their support. If you want more legacies, cultivate your donors so that they truly share your values, then ask them to consider leaving a gift when they die. If you want more clients – beneficiaries of your services – then advertise what you do and ask them to make contact, or go through intermediaries such as medical staff. If you want to influence the government, learn to lobby effectively. If you want more people to support your campaign, again, show them in ads exactly what you want them to do for this campaign and what you believe the outcome will be. This is not rocket science; it's the result of charity brands being significantly different to commercial brands.

7.4.1 Getting re-branding wrong… and right

I know of one UK charity that did a major re-brand and never once consulted its fundraisers. The Director of Fundraising was on maternity leave at the time but such crass stupidity defies understanding. Another charity I know was aware that it was under-performing in its fundraising and decided to re-brand to improve this aspect of its wonderful work. The trustees' decision was clear – we do this but only on the basis that fundraising will improve.

Knowing nothing of such things, the Chief Executive appointed a commercial advertising agency to do the re-brand and recruited someone who had never worked in a charity as the senior staff member responsible for directing the process. Neither agency nor the senior staff member knew anything about fundraising. In fact, I got the feeling they all thought it was rather a grubby occupation!

Several years later, the outcome is clear – fundraised income has actually gone down. Yet word on the street, soon after the event, was that the exercise had met all the charity's 'awareness building' objectives. But that wasn't the brief the trustees had set, though it's a common response when re-branding has failed to achieve the planned increase in fundraised income.

In contrast, you only have to look at the truly awesome impact of major brand changes in UK charities such as Dogs Trust (from the quaintly named National Canine Defence League in 2003) and Macmillan Cancer Support (from Macmillan Cancer Relief in 2004). These are well-documented success stories, and have a number of factors in common.

- The purpose of each re-branding exercise was clear from the start and everybody was focused on it
- They both used major branding agencies, who clearly understood the challenges imposed when working with charity brands
- The process had buy-in throughout the organisation (not always easy to achieve)
- Fundraising was the prime motivator
- …though in the case of Macmillan, bringing its services to new clients with cancer was another major objective.

In both cases the results are impressive. Chief Executive of Dogs Trust, Adrian Burder reported in April 2014 a 250% increase in spontaneous awareness in the previous 10 years. In more practical terms, its voluntary income in 2003 was nearly £19 million. In 2013, it was £72 million – it had grown nearly four times in just 10 years. This was not solely the result of a re-brand. But the energy and focus that a well-run exercise can bring, the inspiration to take the brand to the market, drives fundraising success. And results follow.

Macmillan too has seen staggering success and has become a British 'treasure'. Its income prior to the re-brand was £63 million. Nine years later, in 2013, it raised £187 million. What an example for us all.

There is nothing wrong with re-branding; in fact it can be a opportunity to create success and the discipline can be transformational. And when you have a name like the National Canine Defence League (research showed that many people thought they rescued cats!), or the Distressed Gentlefolk Aid Association, or the Royal United Kingdom Beneficent Association (it became Independent Age), then you certainly need a name-change. But for every well-executed re-branding exercise, there are dozens of examples of money thrown away, with the only outcome a questionable research paper reporting an increase in 'public awareness' of the charity.

If you are going to re-brand, then do the job properly. In the UK there are several experienced commercial brand agencies who have achieved superb charity re-brands. Experience is essential, as is absolute clarity as to the purpose of the exercise. In the next chapter, I will re-affirm the immense power of fundraisers to influence public awareness and to build a brand that is truly loved.

Stephen's rant 9

Why have I spent a whole chapter on the re-branding of charities when most readers of this book are fundraisers and will never go through such an exercise in their careers?

Many communications staff in charities (the ones who work in departments specifically called the communications department or the marketing department) see re-branding as a means to extend their power-base in relation to fundraising staff. Sadly, in some charities, the enmity between these two departments is considerable. Such hostility is a disaster, based as it is on the dichotomy between power and budgets – communications people have the power of message control but little budget; fundraisers have big budgets (with large sums to raise) but have to work with constraints on their messaging imposed by the communications department.

In many charities, the primary role of communications is to campaign for change. In the organisations that get it wrong, campaigning is run as a separate department from fundraising, and, very often, as a separate fiefdom. Such madness is addressed in Chapter 11, when I highlight how the best campaigning charities run both activities closely together adding greatly to both campaigning and fundraising.

Fundraisers have largely acquiesced in discussions to do with re-branding, impressed often by what is no more than brand glitter. It's time this stopped; it's time fundraisers stamped their feet and said: 'If we do not have a major influence on the new brand, then we will no longer be able to raise the money required for this charity to operate'. And they should be prepared to put their jobs on the line for it.

Communications staff are essential in most large charities. But in those where there is no communications task beyond raising money – and that's the majority – communications staff should report to the same directorate as fundraisers. Without question.

8 A happier state, within the power of fundraisers to create

In 2002, Kevin Roberts, CEO Worldwide of Saatchi and Saatchi, published 'Lovemarks – the future beyond brands'[9]. It's a book aimed at the commercial sector and in its sequel 'The Lovemarks Effect'[10] (2006) there is adulation from the leaders of Benetton, Wal-Mart, Ben & Jerry's, Diesel, Proctor & Gamble and so on. There is no reference to charities in Lovemarks and only one charity's name even appears.

But this is still such an interesting book for fundraisers. It looks at what makes a specific brand, one of the many we use and ignore every day, suddenly so important in our lives that it undergoes a metamorphosis. Roberts describes this new entity as a Lovemark. He sat down in his London and US agencies and got his staff to list the brands that have a major impact in their lives. For each person, this is unlikely to number more than perhaps two or three. Here is the list they produced:

Amazon	Harley-Davidson	Nokia
Apple	Italy	Pampers
The Body Shop	LEGO	Red Cross
CNN	Levi's	Swatch
Coca Cola	McDonald's	Toyota
Disney	Manchester United	Vespa
Dyson	Nelson Mandela	Virgin
eBay	Nike	
Google	Nintendo	

9 Roberts K. (2002) 'Lovemarks – the future beyond brands'. PowerHouse Books, New York.
10 Roberts K. (2007) 'The Lovemarks Effect: Winning In The Consumer Revolution'. Powerhouse Books, New York.

You'll know these names, though maybe only one or two will have any impact on you. For me, what leapt out was Apple. I'm writing this on my MacBook Pro. Even now, when I get on the train, I get out my Mac to do some work and 'glance around' casually (and with infinite superiority!) at my benighted fellow travellers with their PCs. My belief in Apple is not simply that I've swallowed the Steve Jobs story. My Mac is everything to me. It doesn't let me down when I stand up to give a presentation. It holds tens of thousands of photographs from both work and family and hundreds of charity TV ads. My Mac is part of me. Apple is a Lovemark for me.

You get the idea. In his book, Roberts describes the quartiles produced by two axes, respect and love. So a product with low levels of each is just a commodity, sold on price. Low respect but high love is a fad, it doesn't last. High respect but low love, well that's a brand. But high levels of both, Roberts calls a Lovemark.

The British Red Cross appeared in the Lovemark list of those within Saatchi who were asked for their views. I can understand that. But just think what it might be like if your charity were to be on the Lovemark lists of large numbers of your supporters – that would be something! The loyalty generated would be hugely influential, let alone the legacy income received decades later.

So what, according to Roberts, makes a Lovemark, and could a charity achieve that status in the affections of large numbers of its supporters? Lovemarks have three key attributes – **mystery**, **sensuality** and **intimacy**. Roberts is talking about commercial products – paint, financial products, games, IT stuff. Yet he is using words that evoke deep, deep emotions about products that most of us would see as merely functional.

In contrast, just think how attractive your charity could become, simply by presenting your life-changing work in ways that **really** engage and satisfy your supporters.

8.1 Mystery

Mystery has five elements and in all of them, charities can really deliver.

First, **'Tell your stories'.** Charities have stories that can move the hardest of hearts; examples of bravery, sadness, injustice and outrage, strength and persistence. The emotions that charities can create are unmatched in any other marketing sphere.

I remember struggling once with a group from a disability charity. We were using the Four Pillars Exercise© to look for the charity's core fundraising proposition, but were wallowing in a sea of political correctness. I changed tack and asked each of my 15 or so charity colleagues to spend a few minutes thinking of one story they had heard from within the charity that had moved them.

We went round the table. By the end, there was barely a dry eye in the room. All our discussions over how to describe the work were thrown out in favour of letting the achievements of the disabled clients tell their own story; achievements made easier (just a little!) by the work of that charity.

Three times a year I receive a simple newsletter from a charity called The Camphill Family. It runs a series of multiple-ability, self-sufficient communities that work like villages. Each newsletter is like a soap opera. It tells stories of people sharing their life together, the ups and downs and the joy of communal life. In one you might read that the sow is in-pig, in the next you find she's produced eight piglets. Great stuff. I feel so wrapped up in the stories of this charity's work, it would be difficult for me to cancel my monthly bank payment.

Second, **'Use your past, present and future'.** Roberts was talking about commercial things, but what jewels we have in the charity world. All charities were inspired and created by individuals, most of them charismatic, energetic and hugely principled. So all charities have a romantic past. Both The Royal British Legion and The Salvation Army raise huge sums on just this basis. Both remind people of long-established values – the former, values of nationhood, courage and sacrifice; the latter, values of goodness, care, love and commitment.

Next, **'Tap into dreams'.** All charities have dreams, though they are more likely to call them Vision Statements, which immediately makes them more difficult to articulate. NSPCC had a dream some years ago, the simplest of dreams: 'Cruelty to children must stop, FULL STOP'. For 10 years its fundraising flourished, just because it articulated a dream that everyone could share. Genius!

Robert's fourth mystery element is **'Nurture your myths'**. The RNLI's iconic picture of the slit-eyed, bearded lifeboatman is just such a 'myth'. In this context, we mean myth as in mythological – full of romance, strength, power and so on. Similarly, images from Médecin Sans Frontières show heroic medical staff (women scored better then men when we tested the images) battling to save someone's life in spite of ghastly conditions. 'Myths' can be charity staff or clients – anything where heroism is clearly on display – and it can be the heroism of the dedicated, white-coated researcher as much as the caring nurse, sympathetic helpline operator or committed teacher.

His last mystery factor is **'Build on inspiration'.** Supporters want to be inspired. They get nothing else from their charitable gift, so a feeling of inspiration and a gift 'well made' is crucial if they are to give again. Charities can do this incredibly easily. If you are a fundraiser, ask yourself: 'What inspires me to come to work every day?' That inspiration must be bottled and purified, then delivered to the supporters. If nothing inspires you, then get out and do something else!

8.2 Sensuality

What a great word, indeed, an astonishing word for Roberts to use, encouraging companies to seek 'sensuality' when marketing commercial products. What he actually meant was 'exploit people's senses', all of them. Not just sight and hearing but touch, smell and taste as well. Again, charities can use the senses better than any commercial company.

Fundraisers need to fulfil the emotional needs of their supporters, and an unrivalled way to reach their emotions is through the senses. Sight and hearing are well-catered for with email and the internet, with rich media embedded into messages, as well as through print, TV and radio. The opportunities are truly inspiring and some charities, such as the RSPB with the webcams on spring nesting birds, are streaking ahead in the race to engage their supporters in the work their donation is making possible.

But you can appeal to other senses as well. For example, since 1998, The Royal British Legion has been sending out masses of small wooden remembrance crosses with a poppy attached. The Legion is closely linked with Britain's armed forces but these crosses are no longer restricted to people who have served. Between one and two million go out every year to current supporters and cold audiences. You can imagine recipients touching them, holding them before writing a name and a short message of remembrance on the back and returning them. Over a hundred thousand crosses are returned. The task of planting them in the grounds of Westminster Abbey, Royal Wootton Bassett, Cardiff Cathedral and other sites in the UK is onerous, but the sight is truly moving. The Queen and thousands of others come to pay tribute to the lives lost and bravery shown.

Truly, this is 'sensuality' working at its best. Supporters' own memories are being given an outlet, in this case focused on a small, remembrance cross that can be held, a name added, and sent on to be planted in a public place.

One of my most effective cold recruitment mailings ever (though it was expensive) was for the charity Sense, which supports people who have neither sight nor hearing. It's a 'difficult' cause to raise money for, because the disabilities are so challenging. The mailing enclosed a small packet of potpourri (hence the expense) with the simple explanation that smell is vital if other senses have been lost. The appeal used sensuality beautifully.

8.3 Intimacy

Roberts describes intimacy as having three parts – commitment, empathy and passion. It is so important for charities to show their supporters (and expect their supporters to show them) commitment, empathy and passion. It is so fundamental to everything a charity should be doing.

Stephen's rant 10

So often, I experience fundraisers with significant expectations of their supporters; expectations that they will respond to an appeal, turn out to an event and so on. But there is considerably less evidence of fundraisers delivering similar commitment, empathy and passion back to their supporters. Take my example of a 'money-back guarantee' for instance (Section 5.3). If you ask fundraisers why they don't do it, their most likely response is to cite the 'administrative difficulties' of running such a scheme. That is the antithesis of 'commitment to supporters'.

To give a practical example from the commercial world, which has for two decades now recognised the need to show customers commitment and empathy, and absolute passion for its product. I contacted an online bank a few years ago for information on how to set up a current account. I then watched as they pursued me for my custom. My initial mailing came back within days (it had to be a mailing because there were forms to complete). It was creatively designed and amusing. This was a bank, yet it was funny! Then over the next year I received eight more letters, all of them amusing, all of them right on-brand and all offering me increasing encouragement to become a customer.

Would a charity deal with a prospective supporter that way? Be in no doubt, the bank did it because it knew it was still profitable long term, to send me nine mailings. Most charities don't even know that sort of information and don't think that way. They should; they must start now.

The best charities nowadays have clear first-year programmes. Better still, they have programmes for the first 15 or 18 months for every supporter, and these vary, depending on the first method or medium of support. There are different plans for supporters who make a cash donation or start a regular monthly gift through their bank, with separate approaches if they do it on- or offline. Those who take part in an event or buy a prize draw ticket, donate goods to a shop or join in a campaign will all be treated differently.

These programmes have many objectives but three important ones. Number one is to achieve a second support activity. You cannot begin to call this new donor a supporter until they have given you another gift or done something else that indicates they believe in your work. Number two is that they must begin to believe that you are thinking of them personally and you share their passion for and commitment to your charity's work. Number three is to move the supporter to the relationship that pleases the supporter best and delivers the most money to the charity, always remembering that a legacy gift is likely to transcend any donation in a supporter's lifetime.

Sending out multiple emails and mailings in the hope that one or two might produce a response doesn't work any more. But sadly, that is what usually happens, and donors do not feel loved.

An example of how to do it well is the online bank I mentioned earlier. In one of its many brilliant TV ads, a charming couple are sitting, talking about what the bank means to them in their life. They talk about their 'feelings' at having such flexible and helpful products from their bank and finish with the inimitable words: 'If you had a pet as good as XXX Bank, you'd feed it chicken and let it sleep on the bed at night'. This is what Kevin Roberts meant when he proclaimed 'Intimacy' as one of the three attributes of a Lovemark.

In 2003, I was speaking about this concept at the staff conference of a major charity. Afterwards, the Chair of Trustees quite casually said: 'Why can't we make our charity into a Lovemark?' The charity was Macmillan Cancer Relief, now Macmillan Cancer Support. And, for me and many others, that charity is now a Lovemark. It's ubiquitous, it steps into families when their lives seem to be collapsing, and through its strong brand it breathes warmth and welcome. It's taken a good number of years, of course, but its vision and focus have never dimmed. And it's not simply the product of a large budget; it comes from a clarity of purpose and huge determination.

9 Creating great fundraising

In this chapter, I feature two keys to great creative expression and show how you can be sure you've got it right. Use the keys, and your income will be transformed. Ignore them, and you'll continue to look for reasons why your fundraising from Minor Donors isn't doing as well as other charities. Donors love great fundraising creative – we know that from their response. They hate – and respond a lot less to – boring stuff that all looks the same.

9.1 The keys to great creativity in fundraising copy

People give to a charity because of two things – they are moved at the plight of those the charity works with, and they are persuaded that, with their help, the charity is able to do something about it. The first is based entirely on emotion and the second is a mix of emotion and reason. But emotion is the main driver of support.

Professor of Neurology at the University of British Columbia, Donald Calne said: 'The essential difference between emotion and reason is that emotion leads to action and reason leads to conclusions.'

Fundraisers are in the **action** business; we need someone to respond with their support. Discussion and agreement from Minor Donors do not produce donations.

Yet, throughout the world, I see appeals that are devoid of emotion. What is worse, they break every fundraising principle ever established. I have already given you my number one fundraising principle: 'Nobody is interested in what your charity does, only in what it achieves when it does it'.

Second on my list is: 'People give to people and only one or two people at that, not masses of them'. It's a well-known principle, yet fundraisers break it all the time.

Practical tips 8

The following are examples of poor fundraising you can spot a mile off:

- The appeal letter has a picture of the Chief Executive – I guarantee that in the copy he will be talking about himself (and it's nearly always a man!) and his charity's work. Nobody is interested in the Chief Executive, nor the charity's work. They only care about what happens when the charity does its work and delivers the outcome

- The appeal letter is a few paragraphs, no more than a single page in length. There is no way any letter can explain the problem that needs a solution, the importance of the problem, what the charity is doing to solve it, what the donor's gift will achieve if it's given to the charity, and how the life of the people will be changed because of it… all on one page. There is one obvious exception to this of course. Where the appeal is asking for donations for a disaster, where that disaster is all over the papers and the TV, the letter can be very short, purely administrative, simply saying: 'We're there, please send us money now'

- On the first page of the letter, the donor is told that thousands, hundreds of thousands or even millions of people are suffering. Madness! A donation from a Minor Donor cannot help thousands of suffering people. It could help one or two of them, or a family, but not thousands. By talking in terms of big numbers, the donor is made to feel helpless and ineffective. That's not a good feeling; the donor will not feel loved.

▨ *Stephen's rant 11*

Contrast the words used in a disaster appeal from two charities – America's International Rescue Committee (IRC) and the UK's Save the Children. They look pretty standard – a short letter, sent in a bright envelope with a simple donation form.

The IRC letter starts: 'The flooding in Pakistan is one of the worst disasters in that country's history. It is also an extraordinary challenge for the IRC.' And a little further down, 'Over 10 million people affected, one fifth of the country under water, well over 500,000 homes destroyed.' Just think about those numbers. You might have responded with a generous donation of $100 or even $500, but, given the scale of the numbers highlighted, you realise it would have little impact. So you don't bother.

In contrast, the Save the Children letter shows the picture of a baby and starts: 'Ibrahim is six weeks old and is already severely malnourished. Without help he will die. But actually, he's one of the lucky ones, he made it to a Save the Children supported hospital.' It then asks you for a generous gift and your heart tells you to do it because it will, at least, help Ibrahim or another kid like him.

Other parts of the IRC's letter are just plain stupid: 'It's also an extraordinary challenge for the IRC.' That says to me that the IRC will rise to the challenge and deliver on its support for Pakistan… with or without my help! Yet people give to people, not to charities, particularly when there's an emergency.

I now add a third, simple fundraising principle. When you are writing fundraising copy, the word 'you' (you, the donor) is so much more important that the word 'we' (we, the charity). This has been articulated by many wonderful fundraising copywriters, particularly by the sublime Tom Ahern, who is American, Virginia-based and the author of another very perceptive thought I'll come on to in a while.

Take the line: 'With your kind gift, we will be able to find children like Ibrahim in the refugee camps, we'll give them special emergency food and restore them to full health'. Actually, it's a reasonably good line. But even in this simple line, the charity gets in the way. In contrast, why not say: 'With your kind gift, you can make sure children like Ibrahim in the refugee camps are given special emergency food and restored to full health'.

All too often the charity prevents the emotional connection between the donor and the recipient.

Practical tips 9

Here's two ways you can spot poor fundraising copy:

Spot the times you use the phrase '…give us a donation and we will…'. Most charities use it all the time. Just replace it with 'Your donation will…'.

Take the letter or email that asks for a gift, count the number of times we, I or the charity's name appears and then count the times you or your is used. On the first page of the IRC's letter (see my rant above), there were 11 of the former and only three of the latter. At worst, the two groups should be about equal. At best, there will be many more uses of you than we.

In talking about those you's and we's, Tom Ahern has articulated another real dilemma that explains why so many charities get the you/we balance wrong. I think this is so perceptive. He explains it like this:

'The way communications departments talk about the work and the way fundraising departments talk about it, are 180 degrees different. The favourite pronoun of communications colleagues is **we**. Their job is to tell the public or the Government or whoever will listen how good the charity is, how effective, how influential, how far-reaching and so on.

'The favourite pronoun of the fundraiser is the opposite, it is **you**. So the fundraiser's job is to sideline the charity and talk about the impact of you, the donor.'

> This is why, if we were talking about Ibrahim, we would write 'With your kind support, you have ensured that children like little Ibrahim….'

9.2 Getting the creative right

Here are guidelines to structure your fundraising stories or help you judge whether the creative you've been given is likely to deliver donations. Good copy needs to have a 'big idea', to demonstrate the need and how you can meet it, to be dramatic, and to delight potential donors.

9.2.1 A 'big idea'

The first essential element of good fundraising copy applies to any creative message, whether it's selling a product or idea. In his 1983 book 'On Advertising', David Ogilvy created the concept of the 'big idea' in advertising. He said: 'It takes a big idea to attract the attention of consumers and get them to buy your product. Unless your advertising contains a big idea, it will pass like a ship in the night. I doubt if more than one campaign in a hundred contains a big idea.'

Ogilvy was a passionate advocate of direct response advertising – direct marketing as we now call it – and his thinking is as apt today as it was then, and as relevant to fundraising as it is to any other sector.

If you are asking people for support for your cause, then you need a 'big idea' for them to grasp. With what, exactly, do you want them to engage their emotions? Let me give you three examples of 'big ideas' that turned out to be huge. One of the best ever is still working 20 years after it was created by Burnett Associates. I suspect it's been printed three or four hundred million times because it's been the slogan for WaterAid through most of its life. The headline reads: 'Give water. Give life. Give £2 per month.' Why is this so good? Why has it prevailed in spite of dozens of alternative creative treatments being tested against it?

In just eight words and for the price of just £2 per month, it says **you** can be god-like and give life. That is **such** a 'big idea'. It is brilliant and because of that, it has lasted and lasted, working on advertisements, inserts, direct mail – everything.

The second is an advertisement by the Royal United Kingdom Beneficent Association (now Independent Age). Here it is the combination of words and a sublime picture that creates the impact. '75 is no age to be leaving home' says the headline and in the picture, an old woman struggles to carry her few possessions. Such passion, such emotion! It is incredibly hard to make printed advertisements work. This one ran successfully for years.

The last is a TV advertisement. When two large cancer charities merged in 2002 to form Cancer Research UK, they created a beautiful advertisement based on the idea of a 'magic mirror'. When you look in a magic mirror, you see loved ones who have died. And to the sound of Eva Cassidy singing, they showed three people who had lost the battle against cancer. Then you saw, in the mirror, a young girl with her mother. I remember the feeling in my stomach: 'Don't tell me the child has died as well'. But the child had survived through the pioneering work of Cancer Research UK. It was a stunning advertisement, **because** it had a big idea.

Ogilvy was adamant: if there is no big idea, tear it up and start again. He lived in a world where budgets didn't matter. In our world, of course, they're rather more important.

So whenever you see a piece of charity creative ask yourself: 'Do I understand clearly and straight away, what difference my money will make if I make a donation?' If you do, then the creative has an idea that is big enough.

9.2.2 Demonstration

Charity creative must show clear need and obvious solutions that supporters can believe in and contribute to. And as discussed earlier, it has to be 'important' in my mind as a supporter, not simply in your mind as a charity. Where there are major emergencies round the world, the needs are obvious and all charities have to do is demonstrate that they are on the ground and operating effectively. This is why charities like Oxfam have a simple, quick-to-produce format for emergency appeals that goes out very soon after an earthquake, flood or other disaster.

Other charities are not in this position. Their appeals have to demonstrate the need. So the very successful Smile Train shows pictures of children with cleft lips and palates that need repair. Habitat for Humanity shows the need with dark, grim, black and white pictures but then provides the solution with a short statement: '100 simple acts of kindness could buy a decent home for an Ethiopian family'. The endearing thing about this appeal is the push-out model house made of card that shows the building that my donation will help to make possible. The sum asked for is just £10.47, and it says it takes just 100 people – £1,047 – to build a Habitat for Humanity house. Wow!

Other charities struggle to demonstrate need; they try to intellectualise their appeals relying on politically correct, rational explanations. These don't work, they never work; don't do them, ever. Fundraising is an emotional business and very simple – supporters will give if you demonstrate need and effective solutions to that need. Provided, of course, they believe you.

In an appeal for the wonderful WWF, the plight of the snow leopard was highlighted. Beautiful pictures on the outer envelope and inside showed these stunning creatures. But the headline was completely spurious: 'This letter contains 300 words. That's one for every snow leopard left in Nepal'. Only writers ever think in terms of word counts. How would anyone else relate such an emotional disaster to such a specialist, indeed, intellectual concept? I would rather learn more about WWF's solutions to the problem than think about the meaning of a 'clever' simile.

In fact, it's rare that 'clever' works, unless the cleverness is used to demonstrate either need or solution.

9.2.3 Drama

However well you describe the need and its solution, your appeal needs emotional drama. For example, in contrast to its Snow Leopard appeal, WWF produced a superb example some years ago. The package was thick, wrapped in polythene, and the words implied that it contained Genuine Powdered Sumatran Tiger Bone. I was outraged, so angry that I should have been sent tiger bone powder. Of course, as I opened the package, unfolded the A2 sheet of paper and learned it was from WWF, my shock that I might have been sent powdered tiger bone was neatly channeled into anger that anyone would trade in this stuff. The appeal asked for support to fight those guilty of trading. Now, that is drama; a truly brilliant use of my own outrage at people who were trading in endangered species.

Another example is an appeal we produced for the UK charity supporting blind and partially-sighted people, the RNIB, to raise money for a confidential reading service for blind people. The appeal came out as an official-looking brown enveloped letter marked 'Private & Confidential'. But it had been ripped open and placed in a plastic envelope for delivery. Anyone picking it up off their doormat would be furious that someone might have read their private correspondence. Once the supporter had felt their own anger at this breach of confidentiality, it was easy to explain what blind people must feel having to have their private correspondence read to them.

Amusingly, when we tried to use this very successful donor mailing to recruit new donors (with the implication that we might be sending out many hundreds of thousands of them), Royal Mail made it clear it didn't want to be blamed for ripping open private correspondence and would not be pleased to see any more in the system!

I offer just one more superb example, from the Zurich-based agency, Spinas Civil Voices for the charity Helvetas. It's a door-drop that goes to houses in Germany, Switzerland and other European countries. It looks water-authority official and says on the outside: 'No water between 29 April and 30 July'. Imagine the anger in each household as recipients rip open the contents. Then the charity explains that a third of the world doesn't have water for three months each year. The anger is channeled into a donation.

Drama can come from a host of clever and relevant ideas: a detailed copy of plans for an extension to a house for people with learning difficulties; a toothbrush, symbolic of everything important that a young teenager might miss if they were forced, through abuse, to run away from home at short notice; a friendship bracelet like the ones made by children with HIV Aids in an African school; or simply a letter, perhaps from a youngster who was abused but is now back on their feet though support from the charity.

It doesn't take much ingenuity to add an important element to make a message come alive for the supporter. With very few exceptions, adding such things into mailings or promising them online will always add to the response. It is the reason some charities have gone over the top and started sending out stuff in envelopes that have absolutely no connection with the appeal – gardening gloves, umbrellas, folders of stationery and so on. These things enhance response, but because they have no relevance to the appeal, they have been outlawed in the Code of Fundraising Practice.

9.2.4 Delight

As a fundraiser, your job is to give the supporter a great experience – to love your donor. Even anger channeled into something positive can be a great experience. There is a host of opportunities to make your appeal delight your audience. For example, you can make it highly relevant to them, perhaps by referring to their cat Smokey or to their previous indications of interest in your charity's work.

The copy for the newspaper advertisement for Elizabeth Finn Care mentioned in Chapter 6 had to do two jobs. It had to find an audience that would understand the fine line that could tip an independent 'professional person' (EFC's client group) into abject and irreversible poverty, then ask them for a gift in their Will. This advertisement was astonishingly successful because it set out to describe the client audience in ways with which potential supporters could easily identify.

'Surprise' is another good form of 'delight'. A long-standing cold recruitment pack for UNICEF was mailed from India, smothered in lovely Indian stamps and printed on scrappy paper stock that UK print machines would spit out. I bet every pack was opened! But inside the appeal was for a factory making toilets. Essential, of course, and when you read the letter you understood just how important this work was.

Then there is always straightforward 'honesty'. I saw a letter written by an Australian fundraiser in answer to someone who had asked what sort of money they should give – a difficult question. She had replied honestly and with real impact: 'Depends! If you are an eccentric millionaire, you might give us $100k in stocks. But if you are 'normal' like me, you'll get more bang out of being a monthly donor – it really adds up! Our average monthly gift is $20/month. I've attached a giving brochure for you if you'd like. Thanks for thinking of us! Siobhan'. This sort of honesty is so refreshing and so caring. Wonderful!

To relevance, surprise and honesty, perhaps you could add 'simplicity'. All these sprinkle the fairy dust of delight on an appeal. You don't need them all and they're not always appropriate, but 'delight' is what fundraisers must aim to give, even with important appeals about difficult subjects.

So, four essentials are needed for good fundraising creative – a big idea (big enough anyway), demonstration, drama and delight. But how do you know you are pushing all the right buttons?

9.2.5 A checklist to make sure you've got it right

The answers to these questions need to be crystal clear to the donor as they read your appeal. If they are not, then you must challenge the copy. I have to thank my long-time friend and business partner Pauline Lockier for this comprehensive checklist of questions the donor has to be able to answer with perfect clarity before they will give a donation:

- Am I clear about the problem?
- Why should I care about this problem?

- What is this charity doing about the problem?
- What do they want me to do as a supporter?
- Why do I need to do it now?
- What happens if I don't send money?
- What proof of success does the charity offer?

9.3 A warning

It's fashionable to believe that appeals don't work as well nowadays as they used to, which explains the rush to ever more flamboyant enclosures in mailpacks and to the increasing use of prize draws as a source of income. There is nothing wrong with prize draws, but they are aimed at a different audience to the supporter who will donate solely because of the power of the need.

Appeals may not always work, but there are usually very good reasons for this. Many fundraisers are not close enough to the work of the charity and struggle to find good case studies. In my view, all fundraisers should spend 5% of their time with the charity's client group; that's just one day per month. When I work with a hospice for instance, case studies abound and that's because the fundraisers work right in the hospice, mixing with patients, relatives and the host of volunteers. In contrast, when I work with large fundraising departments at head office, connection with the work is virtually non-existent.

Without good case studies, there are no stories that will move a supporter and appeals won't work. An example happened in the depths of the autumn 2008 financial crisis in the UK, when Kidney Research UK put out two appeals looking for new donors from the cold recruitment market. The importance of kidney research is not understood by many, so you could argue this is a difficult cause to fundraise for. Each appeal produced an astonishing near-break even response in the cold market. Most charities would expect to lose money acquiring new donors, just as commercial companies lose money finding new customers. Why did these two break even when all around was financial news to chill the soul? Because each was clever, beautifully written and based on a stunning story.

In the first, a mother described how she had been forced to plan her child's funeral… before she had even given birth. The boy was born and lasted a matter of minutes before his kidney malfunction kicked in. The mother was appealing for research funds to prevent this happening to others. I was near to tears when I read that copy.

In the second, the appeal letter was from the failing kidney to the little girl with kidney disease. It didn't touch me at all, but it was charming and sweet and beautifully written and clearly moved many others. Both appeals were successful simply because the fundraisers at this dynamic charity knew how to find good stories.

The next chapter focuses on the most important supporter relationship any fundraiser will have – the relationship with someone who has pledged a legacy.

10 The ultimate goal, a legacy gift

In a book where I have not touched on any particular medium and steered away from 'technique', why am I singling out one aspect of fundraising – legacy marketing – and devoting a whole chapter to it? There are many reasons, but the main ones are:

- The sums involved are so huge, the impact of this money is so transforming, that it transcends **any** other form of fundraising. All but the biggest major gifts are chicken feed in comparison to legacies. Regular monthly gifts paid through the bank – legacies dwarf even this welcome source of money. Corporate gifts are but pennies in a bucket

- Yet people in charities (not, thankfully, the fundraisers) don't take legacy marketing seriously at all. Many trustees and senior charity staff believe legacies are the gift of the legacy fairies, they are that complacent. They love the money flowing in but don't seem to think the flow can be promoted nor that it might stop one day without such promotion. Which is why in so many charities, legacy income remains the responsibility of the finance department – disaster! And it's why so little research has been done in this vital field

- Legacy marketing is not done very well even in UK, which probably leads the world in this form of fundraising

- Most important of all, if you get your legacy marketing right, the satisfaction you give to your supporters can be the most profound, and the relationship with such golden supporters, quite the deepest you'll ever create. Offering your donors the opportunity to leave your charity a gift when they die could be the greatest expression of their commitment to you. Can that be done by one man and a dog in a backroom in a finance department? No, it can't, and it's time all charities woke up to the fact.

Of course, there are many that have done so already (woken up that is!) but there are others for whom the flow of legacy income is still steady without much effort. They are walking a tightrope. Legacy marketing started in UK in 1986 with the iconic WWF advertisements created by my long-time friend and business partner, Nick Thomas. The two advertisements have since become the stuff of legends. One read: 'More men are guilty of intestacy than adultery', and the other: 'More women are the victims of intestacy than rape'. Intestacy is dying without a Will. It was bold for a charity that was, at the time, well established but by no means in the mainstream and popular position it occupies now.

But now in the UK, every charity, museum, political party, hospice, theatre, university and school is trying its hand at legacy marketing and the 'free money' that has traditionally flowed into the big national charities will be diverted elsewhere unless they do something to secure it.

10.1 The vast sums involved

The figures are truly stupendous. In the UK, in the 10 years to 2011, the money left in legacies to charities varied between £1.7 billion and £2.1 billion[11]. The largest UK charity, Cancer Research UK, received 33.3% of its income in 2013/14 from legacies – a total of £163 million. In 2012/13, our biggest animal charity, the RSPCA, derived 51% of its funding – £67.7 million – from people who had died. So this money is in every sense 'life-changing'. Huge amounts of charitable work would not get done were it not for gifts in supporters' Wills.

The average value of a legacy in the UK is currently around £19,500; in the US it is about $37,000. But there are two more interesting UK average values for 2013 from

11 NCVO (2014). 'UK Civil Society Almanac 2014'. NCVO, London

the company Legacy Foresight, based on its excellent Legacy Monitor Consortium – a group of 67 major charities that account for roughly half the UK's legacy income. These are estimates for all UK charities and show the average residuary legacy (the value of the balance of the estate after all other payments have been made) was £40,000, and the average pecuniary legacy (a specific sum named by the person who has died), was £2,600.

At £40,000, the average UK residuary legacy is a serious sum of money, the sort of sum that would have a charity's major gift fundraisers scurrying for the Chief Executive and Director of Services, Science or whatever. Meetings would be arranged, the charity's 'senior team' would swing into action and fundraisers rightly congratulated when the major gift was secured.

Why does the same 'senior team' show such indifference to legacy marketing? Let me tell you a tale to encourage CEOs and senior directors to get involved. I had a conversation with the Chief Executive of a middle-sized charity about starting a legacy campaign. With some trepidation, I suggested it would benefit hugely from the support of a Board 'champion', a trustee willing to drive the campaign forward. The trouble was, I explained, it would be important that the 'champion' should be able to say 'I have changed my Will, and I'm leaving a gift to this charity'.

'That's all right,' said my CEO, 'I'll get all of them to change their Wills in our favour before we even start the campaign!!'

If she succeeds, it will surely be a first. And what a triumph! I can think of no more powerful statement of the importance of legacies to a charity than to have all the trustees signed up.

So, here's a big question. Are there really supporters out there who could be encouraged to leave a gift in their Will to their favourite charity? Of course there are! Research by the Institute of Fundraising's legacy promotion consortium, Remember a Charity, showed a considerable gap between those who say they are happy to give a small percentage of their estate as a gift to a charity (at an exciting 35%) and those who actually do (at a depressing 6%)[12]. Only a change of culture (the task that Remember a Charity is bravely tackling) and the marketing efforts of individual

12 TNS research for Remember a Charity (2008)

charities will narrow that gap.

In the UK in 2013, the value of legacies was down in real terms since a peak in 2008, largely due to depressed house prices and a poor stock market. But the number of legacies being left to charities is going up, no doubt the result of that gradual change of culture encouraged by the visionary Remember a Charity campaign. Probate – the official proving of a Will – is required on estates valued at £15,000 or more. It is an exciting fact that the percentage of Wills that now go to probate with a charitable gift has increased from 12.2% in 2007 to 14.4% in 2012[13]. This is very good news; long may it continue.

But still, within charities, the interest in legacy marketing is negligible. Why? It's almost as if it's unseemly, somehow grubby, to ask older people for a gift in their Will. But of course, few CEOs and trustees, and virtually no service delivery directors, ever talk to older supporters, in spite of them being 'Major Donors in waiting'. And that distaste, transmitted through the charity, has meant that many legacy marketing materials – in contrast to the sophistication of other forms of Minor Donor fundraising – have until quite recently been very poor.

10.2 Quality research badly needed

A major reason senior managers are indifferent is that, unlike general fundraising, very little research has been done into supporters' motives for leaving a gift in their Will, the trigger points that encourage it and how they can be predicted, the influence of age, gender, religious belief and dozens of other issues. So much needs to be researched, so little has yet been done. And of course such research offers multiple challenges; not least, the fact that the supporter leaving the legacy is dead!

Research can be carried out with supporters who have pledged a legacy, but this is not something that can be tackled lightly in a focus group – a legacy is deeply felt and highly personal. The outcome of the research, of course, is unique to the nation in which it is conducted. Unlike other aspects of fundraising, legacy marketing must reflect the norms of the society. The UK is way ahead of other nations in the boldness

13 Figures by kind permission of Smee and Ford legacy specialists

with which charities ask their supporters for a gift in their Wills; elsewhere this would be unacceptable. But if you raise money in a country that finds such legacy asks intrusive, do remember that, in the UK, such asks only appeared in 1986 with the two WWF advertisements mentioned above. That's not long ago, and it was deemed pretty outrageous at the time. Now every charity asks for a legacy gift; it is normal and completely accepted by supporters.

For the first 20 years of legacy marketing, UK charities went out to their supporters with offers of free 'How to make a Will' guides. It was an easy way to start. At the time it was known that large numbers of British people died intestate, so there was logic in trying to offer such guides, but the thinking was naïve.

Charity supporters are different from the general British public, particularly those who see an ad or a mailing, and bother to read it, make a donation and post it off. These are, by nature, careful folk who expect to contribute more to society than they get out of it. And as they get older, these careful, socially-aware people do what they know they should – they make their Wills. In fact, in 2002, Adrian Sargeant, supported by legacy specialist company Smee & Ford[14], approached 1,500 supporters from five charities, all of whom had been exposed to a recent legacy message. He found that 87.6% of them had already written their Will.

So, if any of those charities had sent a booklet saying 'How to make your Will', at most, only 12.4% of the audience would have found it interesting. In the UK, legacy marketing is not about Will-making any more, it is about something much deeper. In other nations, the idea of offering a free booklet may be a more appropriate way to introduce the idea of leaving a gift to the charity.

10.3 Poor creative

The lack of understanding of the target audience has led to some howlers in terms of creative. Remember, most creative folk and many staff responsible for legacy marketing in charities are in their twenties or thirties. So, the first mistake they make when given a brief for a legacy campaign is to ponder on the fact that the audience

---

14 Sargeant A. and Radcliffe R. (2004). 'Successful Legacy Fundraising – Just What Do Donors Think Is Appropriate? 24th International Fundraising Congress, Noordwijkerhout, The Netherlands.

is old. You can see their brains struggling: 'I'm not even writing for my parents' generation, I'm actually writing for my grandparents (or even great-grandparents)'. It is a challenge few can cope with.

The thing they must remember is that the audience is certainly old, but only in terms of years. In their minds, these supporters are still in their thirties or forties. Their energy levels may be a bit low, but they are still passionate about changing the world, just as they were all those years before. They may have lost that passion briefly when kids demanded every ounce of energy, but in later years they are on fire.

So, a booklet covered in fountain pens, lace, magnifying glasses, hat-pins and pearls doesn't resonate with them any more than it would with a 30-year-old. As for quill pens, whoever came up with that as a concept for a legacy booklet? These grandparents are vibrant, excited with life, and computer literate, like everyone else.

The younger generation also struggles with the d…. word – death! They have little experience of it. Older people have got used to the idea, simply because their friends are dying around them. It becomes 'one of those things'. They are comfortable to talk about death and their Will, much happier than most fundraisers are. In the same 2002 research, Adrian Sargeant showed that over three-quarters of the supporters confirmed they were perfectly happy to be asked for a gift in their Will.

Fundraisers are the ones who are embarrassed at such things. How is this demonstrated? More than in any other forms of fundraising, legacy materials tend to mirror each other, which means they all make the same blunders. The reason many fundraisers give for wanting the supporter to tell them they have left their charity a legacy is futile: 'Please let us know, because it will help us plan ahead', they say. Dozens and dozens of charities use this lame reason for wanting a response, lame of course because no charity could ever know when they will receive my legacy!

Then there's the 'Where there's a Will, there's a way' pun! I visualise copywriters wreathed in smiles stumbling onto this old-fashioned phrase, a phrase they would never use in their own conversation, except mockingly. They latch onto it, thinking 'old people' are bound to like the clever play on words. Well they don't, and they don't like the patronising tone that goes with it either.

There was a period when in the UK you could read: 'Are you Willing to save a wood?'; 'The Will to succeed'; 'The Will to fail'; 'The Will to help'; 'The Will to save lives at sea'; and dozens more. Clever copy rarely works and clever puns never do.

I wrote to a hospice recently, asking for information on how my mother's legacy might help. I was cheating of course, I simply wanted to see their material (which was pretty poor!), but I might have been a genuine supporter wanting to leave money to a charity that had meant so much to me. I might have considered this gift because I wanted to make a real difference.

The letter in reply was extraordinary. There were two lines thanking me for expressing an interest in such a gift, then seven lines describing the hospice's start in 1900, a particular gift in 1903 and its official opening in 1905. Why? In the second paragraph of a letter that could yield, say, £25,000 or £50,000, why talk about stuff that happened to the hospice over a century before?

There's another funny thing about hospice legacy fundraising. Many legacy materials from hospices are full of pictures of rooms with empty chairs. Clearly, this is where medical and nursing staff hold sway and refuse to let mere fundraisers take pictures of the patients. But every patient I've ever talked to is thrilled to be able to contribute to the hospice in any way they can, and most will happily take part in a photo shoot.

Take a look at some hospice legacy materials. Where you see pictures of empty chairs in empty rooms, or smiling staff without a patient in sight, there you'll find a fundraiser struggling without support against a patronising management team that is forcing its own prejudices on its elderly patients. Team members should be reminded where their salaries come from; many from the gifts of grateful patients who have died. Patients want to be given the opportunity to donate in this way.

▨ *Stephen's rant 12*

The word 'grammar' might make you fall asleep, but please stay awake for this rant! Having said that older people are really young people whose bodies are slowing down with age, I have to point out that their years have made them 'picky'. Having to reach for the magnifying glass because the legacy information is set in a 10-point typeface annoys them and they won't bother to read it.

And if they spot bad English, they will stop reading the content and start looking for the grammatical howlers. People currently over 60 were taught grammar in their English lessons and remain proud to get it right.

My agency was working with the wonderful Jane Asher on the first Remember A Charity campaign a few years ago and the Account Director was in despair because Ms Asher was so unhappy with the copy that she wanted to write it herself. I looked at it and threw it back: 'I'm not surprised, it's got two split infinitives'. 'What's a split infinitive'? came the reply, and technically the account director was right. Whoever is the arbiter of good English in the UK had decreed only months before that split infinitives were now acceptable!

When we took out the two split infinitives, with a few other minor tweaks, Ms Asher signed off the copy. Jane Asher is my generation, but it's also members of my generation who are currently changing their Wills to leave legacies to charities. If poor grammar is preventing your target audience from getting your message, and it will, then get your grammar right!

10.4 Getting your creative right

The best UK legacy materials are beautifully written, full of stories of tremendous change achieved by the charity, with lives transformed. As yet there is no research-based proof, but recent thinking from Professors Adrian Sargeant and Jen Shang on issues of people's 'identity' has considerable significance. They argue that where there is a clear time gap between the commitment of a gift and its execution (as there is with a legacy gift), there is no point in linking simple statements of need with the giving of a donation that fulfills that need – '£10 makes a blind man see' or 'A monthly gift of £3 pays for essential research', for example.

Sargeant and Shang argue[15] that the longer the time gap, the more essential it is that the supporter is able to match their own life values clearly with those of the charity. So an 'ask' for a gift in a supporter's Will has to be based on outcomes, as with all asks, but these are outcomes of major visionary change or improvement, outcomes that are to do with 'right', 'equality', 'goodness' etc. These are outcomes that display the charity's core values.

What this means in terms of legacy marketing is exciting. The charity must lay out what it stands for, the principles that drive it and the successes that give it legitimacy. This must be done not in a dry description of boring mission and vision statements, but in terms of great work accomplished through support by good people. If ever there was a need for passionate description, this is it, but the emotion must be rooted in clear logical connection with the good the charity is striving to achieve.

Legacy materials are a copywriter's dream and the best of them are an uplifting experience. They have to be, because they are looking for the supporter's largest **ever** gift, their greatest statement of commitment.

It's always astounded me that fundraisers have difficulty finding case studies of supporters who have made such gifts. I don't think they try hard enough, or maybe they are simply embarrassed to ask grieving families about the motives behind a legacy. Many relatives will be proud to explain the feelings that drove their loved-one to leave such a gift. These are the stories (as well as those from supporters who have pledged a legacy) that should fill the supporter's magazine, the legacy materials and every public presentation ever made about the charity.

In the UK, I believe there is no place in legacy materials for Will-making arrangements – lists of things to think about in planning a trip to the lawyer, legislative terms explained and all the other legal rubbish that still fill many legacy materials. Legacy materials must sell the idea of leaving the ultimate gift. The description of how that is achieved is simple: 'Go to your solicitor'. That's all you need.

This may not be so in other countries around the world. Where the impact of a legacy gift on the work of a charity is not so widely understood, or where asking for a gift at all would be socially challenging, then the method we used in the UK in the 1980s

---

15 Sargeant A. and Shang J. (2008) 'Identification, Death and Bequest Giving'. A report to the Association of Fundraising Professionals. www.afpnet.org/files/contentdocuments/Sargeant_Final_Report.pdf.

and 1990s is the better route to travel. Offer your supporters a free guide on 'Making or changing your Will'. And in it you can show the impact of legacy gifts, but diluted by talk of Will-making, lawyers and legal terms.

Meanwhile, supporter magazines must feature regular 'legacy' stories. These could include an article written by the daughter of someone who has just left a legacy, explaining how proud she is that her mother has used her money so wisely even after her death, or one from a couple explaining how their children are now well established, so they are happy to leave a small percentage of what they have to their favourite charities.

'Free Will Weeks' or other devices used by numbers of charities do succeed, because they focus the supporters' minds on something they've been meaning to do for some time and give them impetus. Cancer Research UK (CRUK) is a shining example of forward-thinking and enjoys significant success with its Free Will Weeks. Regularly, the charity visits a town, publicises its Free Will Week and drives supporters and others into the hands of local lawyers who have signed up to the programme and agreed to write Wills for free. It started in 1993 and took just over 10 years and upwards of £12 million before the break-even point was reached when the investment in the scheme was matched by the legacy income resulting directly from it. That is long-term planning. Since that break-even year, 2004, the resulting legacy income has been rocketing exponentially.

Figures for 2011/12 published recently showed cumulative income from this source to be a little short of £70 million at a cost of around £20 million. But the steepness of the ongoing, upward income curve is incredibly impressive.

The scheme is aimed primarily at a cold audience, though no doubt current supporters take advantage of it. But even the impressive CRUK does not make a serious and conspicuous investment into the stewardship of its current donors with the sole aim to develop legacy income. I know – I'm one of them.

But the fact the Will is 'free' will not spur many; you will only earn your gift through the passionate articulation of what you stand for and the outcomes you can show you are able to achieve with serious money.

10.5 A last word on promoting legacies

In the UK, 74% of people support charities but only 6% of them leave a charitable gift in their Wills when they die. Yet 35%, when asked, say they would be happy to leave a 'small amount' to a charity in their Will.

So, in 2000 a group of leading UK charities set up what was then called the Legacy Promotion Campaign, now the Remember a Charity consortium. The model has now been repeated all over the world because the principle is simple. If charities combine to promote the leaving of a legacy, it has more impact than individual charities doing it themselves. Charities continue marketing to their close supporters and volunteers, of course. Initially, marketing was aimed at the general public, but as years went by and commitment to the consortium waned, Remember a Charity homed in on the most important influence on a person's likelihood to leave a gift when they die – a simple reminder from a lawyer.

Recent research by The Cabinet Office Behavioural Insights Team and Charities Aid Foundation[16] shows how key this influence is. In a control group, the lawyer drawing up the Will asked no questions about the client's intention to leave a gift to a charity in their Will. In a test group (Test 1), they simply asked the question: 'Would you like to leave any money to charity in your Will'? In Test 2, they said: 'Many of our clients like to leave money to charity in their will. Are there causes you are passionate about'?

The results are impressive. In the control group, only 4.9% of the clients added a gift to a charity into their Will. In Test 1, the response more than doubled (10.8%), and in Test 2 it was more than three times (15.4%). The impact of that simple question, which most lawyers would be happy to ask, is phenomenal. But that's not all. The research recorded the value of the pecuniary legacy that was then added to the Will. There was no significant difference between the values in the control group and Test 1 – the average was around £3,200. In Test 2, however, the value doubled to £6,661.

Simply referring to 'other clients' doing something that is seen as socially valuable is enough to triple the response rate and double the average value of the money left to a charity. This supports the findings of Professors Adrian Sargeant and Jen Shang in their work on 'social information' – the influence of a reference to other donors in

16 Behavioural Insights Team (2013) 'Applying behavioural insights to charitable giving'. Cabinet Office/Charities Aid Foundation, London. www.gov.uk/government/publications/applying-behavioural-insights-to-charitable-givingf.

the ask, as outlined in Chapter 4.

My agency launched the Legacy Promotion Campaign with ads in the press and on TV. With the benefit of hindsight, I would have ploughed all that money into a series of campaigns to gain the support of probate lawyers. They are key to promoting charities and, while they will not nominate any one charity in particular, most are happy to ask the right question; indeed, you could argue it's part of their brief. It's such a small step. In contrast, as commercial companies understand all too well, it takes massive marketing budgets to change a nation's behaviour, particularly one based on culture. In the charity world, such budgets do not exist.

10.6 Looking after your pledgers

'Pledgers' is a horrible word used to describe truly heroic people who are so passionate about your work they are going to give you a slice of their estate when they die. And they've told you so. Why would they do that?

From a combination of Adrian Sargeant's research in 2003 and research for the Remember a Charity consortium in 2004, I estimate that only about 10 in 25 people will actually tell you. In one sense that's good news because it means that for every 10 responses to a legacy campaign saying they will leave you a gift in their Will, another 15 will do it but not let you know.

That's a pity. You really need to be aware of who these people are, both because you want to judge the success of the legacy campaign, and because you need to keep them in touch with the ongoing impact of your work. You need to put them on a list of supporters who under no circumstances should be abused. Though of course, **all** your supporters should be on that list.

In 2008, the children's charity the NSPCC came up with an innovative approach. It wanted to ask supporters who were committed to leaving a legacy to let the charity know about it. Five times in one appeal it told supporters that there was no need to tell the charity of their decision. Point four of a 10-point 'charter' read: 'You can tell us you've left a gift if you want to, and we'd love to hear, but you don't need to and we won't keep asking'.

What was the outcome of this bold new idea? The NSPCC received significantly more notifications of legacies made. I think that's wonderful. If you assure these feisty but older supporters that they don't need to tell you something deeply personal, they will happily tell you. If you demand that they do tell you, they won't!

One way to encourage supporters to confirm whether they have left you a gift is to suggest you will invite them to special events. The National Trust, The Royal British Legion and several other innovative charities run gatherings of 'pledgers' in really interesting places. They are briefed about the work of the charity, shown around the venue and generally made to feel special.

The National Trust is a great example. Of course, the Trust has stunning properties to show off and supporters are offered fascinating 'behind the scenes' tours. Some 20 events are organised each year to thank supporters who have pledged a legacy and to show them how these gifts will be used. Fifteen other events are run for general Trust members to persuade them to leave a legacy. The participants pay for their day (around £20) and are encouraged to bring a friend. These occasions are over-subscribed many times over.

Marcia Dover, Head of Legacies at the National Trust, has a clear view of what makes these events such a success. It's not just the iconic properties, though they do make a wonderful backdrop. 'My advice [to other fundraisers] is always the same,' she says. 'Find the essence of what makes your charity great, then look at how to present it. Our real secret weapon is the enthusiasm of the staff. Never underestimate the power of a head gardener talking about his job when he loves it so much!'

I've run legacy events for charities and have watched with enormous pride as feisty 70-year-old supporters grill service delivery staff for information. For the first few minutes, the staff don't know what's hit them! They simply don't understand the passion of these supporters for the work they are delivering. But quickly they learn to love it. Long friendships and total commitment are fostered at these events. And there's a spin-off for fundraisers. Suddenly, case studies appear as if by magic: 'I wondered if your supporters might like to hear about…'?

My message is very clear. Supporters who have said they are leaving your charity a gift in their Will are like gold dust. Treat them as well as, if not better, than you would a Major Donor who comes flashing a £50,000 cheque. This means the CEO should take every opportunity to meet them. The Director of Services, Science or whoever should not be far behind and the more pleasure these and other colleagues are able to give these supporters, the more they'll become advocates not only of the charity but of this very special way of supporting it.

Real money follows such a strategy, eclipsing all other voluntary income. Take legacy marketing very, very seriously.

11 The next 10 years – new opportunities

Throughout this book I've tried to avoid the tedious online/offline debate. Naïve and inexperienced people talk about online fundraising taking over the world. And equally, offline fundraising could learn such a lot from the dynamism of online, if people only cared to look – but they don't. Six or seven years ago I was so bored with offline direct marketing fundraising, I was ready to hang up my boots. Now, fundraising has never been so exciting with our new-found ability to provide individual supporters with just the relationship they seem to want.

Yet in most charities, the income brought in online is still pretty small. The only comprehensive figures come from the data company Blackbaud in the US. A hugely authoritative source, these figures should hang on the walls of every fundraising department in the world. Blackbaud's survey of over 3,359 of the biggest charities in the US shows that in 2013, only 6.4% of the income came in online[17]. And that includes people like me who are sent a mailed appeal but respond online.

Only 6.4%, yet in every conference round the world there are five 'online' sessions for every 'offline' session. Why? Because fundraisers are 'young' (in my definition, that's anyone under about 55!), new media are their life-blood and constant companion and they forget that **real** money comes from older people who are less comfortable users of these media.

So, are we perhaps asking the wrong question? Are we expecting too much of what is no more than just a medium? Online's strength is its ability to allow people to engage in ways that please them, before having to think about a financial gift. Never is this more evident than in the wave of two-stage, multi-channel recruitment that

17 Blackbaud (2014) 'Charitable Giving Report: How Nonprofit Fundraising Performed in 2013'. Blackbaud. www.blackbaud.com/nonprofit-resources/charitablegiving

hit the UK in 2013. Its purest form comes with the wonderful political campaigns by Amnesty or Greenpeace. Their posters proclaim some outrage and you are invited to stop it simply by texting a word to a number.

Save the Children's 2009 campaign changed the sector. At the time, Israelis were bombing Palestine and Palestinians were rocketing Israel. Civilians, children, were the ones who were suffering and Save the Children stepped right out of line and produced an advertisement (it only appeared three times) simply saying: 'Enough is enough, text CEASEFIRE to 81819'. It caught perfectly the mood of Britain at the time. The result – 190,000 people texted CEASEFIRE. Phone calls followed and 9.5% of them converted to a regular monthly gift, a staggering story of exceptional (two-stage) fundraising success. These numbers have been discussed on many conference platforms.

This was grown-up multi-channel fundraising at its best. Three advertisements cost perhaps £50,000 or 60,000. If the average gift from the 18,000 supporters recruited to monthly giving was, say, £50 a year (plus Gift Aid), then the annual income generated would exceed £1 million – a massive return on investment. But the real return was the understanding on the part of the British public that here, at last, was a charity that was prepared to stand up against something that was stupid, that was wrong. And Save the Children has never looked back.

Think secondly, of the impact on those who took part in the campaign. I was one of them. I felt good, really good, when a few days later the ceasefire happened. I understand rationally that my text had no impact and if I thought about it, Save the Children had no impact either. But giving and supporting and believing in something important is **nothing** to do with rationale. It is raw emotion. If you don't want to accept that, then get out of fundraising and become an actuary. I quoted Donald Calne in Chapter 9, who said: 'The essential difference between emotion and reason is that emotion leads to action and reason leads to conclusions'. Fundraisers are in the 'action' business.

11.1 The two-stage recruitment phenomenon

In this book I've given two examples of two-stage recruitment based on campaigning. To a fundraiser, the object of the campaign is unimportant. It is the 'emotional engagement' first, followed by the 'ask' that is the essence of this technique. But it is the same in all fundraising – any 'ask' has to have two (or more) stages. It's how your donors want to be loved. Fundraisers must stop demanding money from supporters and, in any 'ask', start by engaging them emotionally first. Then the 'ask' simply becomes an administrative process that confirms the pleasure they feel at helping to change people's lives.

In very simplistic terms, this engagement is a hook to draw people in. Here's another example of a brilliant two-stage engagement. For a decade people have worried about the decline of bee populations. In 2013 Friends of the Earth launched its Bee Project asking for support to force the government to introduce 'bee-friendly' strategies – 'Text BEE to 70123 to give £3'.

But Friends of the Earth was so much more clever. As well as asking for a small gift, with its implication that a phone call would follow shortly afterwards asking for a bigger gift, it offered a packet of 'bee-friendly flower seeds'. So when, inevitably, the follow-up call came, the discussion did not centre on making a monthly gift to the bee cause, but on the contents of the bee-friendly flower seeds. Donors looked forward to the call, happy to give their postal address, because without it, Friends of the Earth couldn't deliver the seeds. The seeds were the hook; the subsequent ask for a monthly gift was a pleasure to deliver.

Let me give you an offline example, technically a one-stage 'ask' but with two clear parts to it – the engagement and the ask. My agency produced a donor mailing for a wonderful UK child cancer charity CLIC Sargeant. This mailing asked for donations to provide support for young children (and their families) going through radiotherapy for leukaemia. We sent out a piece of string asking supporters to hold it as they read the letter. We then explained the importance of this simple string, the only connection between a three-year-old child being treated for cancer in a whirring, noisy machine and mum, stuck the other side of a massive radiation-proof door. The child, lying quite still as required, can give the string a little tug, and mum can respond. Here, the string is the hook.

Providing engagement hooks is simply good fundraising. Many charities ask for money without any attempt to engage the donor first, and donors feel exploited – unloved. That's not good news. The joy of new media is that the hooks can be so personal and often involve a range of different media. In the bee campaign, posters led to a text, to a mobile call, to a mailed package – four different media. And no doubt, Friends of the Earth moved on to use all the multi-channel opportunities we have now.

Here's another, multi-media example from Dublin. For several years my agency worked with the Irish Cancer Society on its annual Daffodil Appeal. The new and dynamic Head of Fundraising at the time (she was American – well, she still is!) had quickly understood the charity was at the mercy of the Irish weather each year (possibly worse even than English weather). One Friday in late March each year, the charity puts an impressive number of volunteers out on the streets of Ireland collecting money in exchange for daffodil badges.

The big question was, what would happen if the day was blighted by gale-force winds and sleeting rain? Sure enough, that's what happened in 2013. The only people on the streets were the volunteers and the money raised was much reduced.

So, to spread the risk and introduce new ways to support this most iconic of Irish charity days, direct marketing fundraising was started, and it was multi-channel. The appeal letters were sent to supporters and inserted with great success into national papers, providing a paper daffodil that could be returned with a message of support for, or in memory of, those fighting cancer. The first paper daffodils were planted in a Garden of Hope in Phoenix Park in Dublin and made a wonderful display. So far this shows nothing new or clever, just effective (and profitable) fundraising. And Gardens of Hope then sprang up round Ireland.

The clever thing was that a virtual garden was created on the web (www.plantadaff. ie) where you could do just the same thing. You didn't have to make a donation, but encouragement to do so was sprinkled throughout the site. You could share your virtual daffodil with a friend and through Facebook, send your friends bunches of (virtual) daffs, a cup of cheering coffee and so on. Several years later and a change of leadership, the online and offline gardens are virtually gone, presumably because they didn't make money. For me, the new leadership has simply missed the point.

11.2 The first, simple step

Getting your donors to use multiple channels makes them much more valuable. Their lifetime value increases the more media they use. So, what might we be doing in five years?

Imagine you respond to a television or mailed appeal from a charity, sending a donation or direct debit form providing a regular monthly gift. You receive a mailed thank-you card but it gives you a personalised URL that connects you online to **your** page on the charity's site. There you can be asked what motivated you to donate, what your interests are, how you want to hear about the work your support is making possible and so on. The thanks can be effusive.

The next appeal you receive can directly reflect your interests. The project now needing your support can be tailored to you, and the promise given of feedback on how your money is changing lives. An overseas charity can provide a Google Earth URL to take you to the area visually.

The project you've chosen may only have a limited number of supporters. You could all be linked together through Facebook or a blog on the site, giving you an opportunity to chat to others supporting the same project. The charity could let you know exciting news of progress or challenge through the same medium. Indeed, maybe one of the supporting group could visit the project, sending back news and photographs.

All this is easy with the new technologies available. So let's take it further. If I am contributing to a healthcare centre overseas for instance, a webcam can be set up to show me **my** Centre – my Centre that is, shared with the others in my group who are all contributing. The key is that I am becoming part of a community working together to achieve something, with the charity simply acting as the catalyst – and the beneficiary.

In the future, a charity's job will be to build communities of supporters who share interests in common. Not everybody will want to join such a group, but increasing numbers will and the trend will continue for a good few years yet. It's the stuff of the future and the first charities to make it work will reap good rewards.

If nothing else, charities should be using email as well as mail, telephone as well as text, small intimate postcards with thanks and online recognition through a range of social media. But it's not happening. There is very little integration – managing social media is often the remit of a communications team rather than a tool of fundraising. Online fundraisers in charities are beating their breasts because online doesn't yet raise much money, when actually it could be doing such good work in creating intimacy and connection with existing and new donors. As a delivery mechanism it is unsurpassed.

11.3 The opportunity to get it wrong is huge

Early in 2010, food manufacturing giant Nestlé was upset by a clever spoof of its Kit Kat ad produced by Greenpeace. It showed a man eating an orang-utang's finger contained in a Kit Kat wrapper. Blood dripped down his face. The campaigning group was complaining that the Nestlé sources of palm oil were devastating virgin forest. On one day, I watched Nestlé's Facebook site explode with angry comments as executives tried to insist on the correct use of its logo, an exercise as futile as re-arranging the deckchairs on the Titanic. It was like a feeding frenzy as potential customers queued up to hurl abuse.

Nestlé's handling of the battle – for battle it was – had not been planned. Its lawyers succeeded in having the video removed from YouTube, so Greenpeace immediately put it on Vimeo and posted that fact on Twitter. Two months, 1.5 million video viewings, 200,000 emails, hundreds of phone calls and countless Facebook posts later, Nestlé capitulated and agreed it would not use palm oil from sources that destroy virgin forest. This was portrayed as a battle between the good guys and the bad guys, run with incredible efficiency on the web by Greenpeace. I've no doubt that Nestlé now has an effective social media strategy to handle such criticism.

But let us not kid ourselves that charities are exempt from critical exposure. There have been a number of cases where a charity has made an announcement, only to be engulfed in criticism that spreads like wildfire through social media. And the immediate consequences of the mishandling of these criticisms include the decimation of fundraised income.

11.4 Expressing yourself in the next 10 years

Everything I've said in this book supports a view that in the next 10 years charities will have to understand their supporters much better and provide for them as near 'individually' as possible. Fundamental to this is an understanding of the emotions that drive supporters' motivation. I want to draw on a paper that I wrote with nfpSynergy's Joe Saxton nearly 20 years ago, which describes a motivational hierarchy through which supporters may pass, encouraged, hopefully, by smart fundraisers. It's a hierarchy that looks a bit like Maslow's Hierarchy of Needs.

Joe repackaged it in 2008 for his excellent nfpSynergy paper: 'A strong charity brand comes from strong beliefs and values'[18], and I think it's more relevant now than at any other time.

The hierarchy has five levels. Starting at the bottom is the motivating pressure of a person's '**local environment**'. By way of illustration, I wouldn't feel comfortable in London in early November if I wasn't wearing a remembrance poppy. But the fact that I put a £1 coin in a box and wear my poppy has nothing to do with my support for The Royal British Legion. Most people make no connection between the poppy and The Legion, in spite of some of the most innovative marketing over the last 15 years. I wear a poppy because it's the right thing to do.

Or I might buy a prize draw ticket sent to me by a charity, but in that case my prime

18 Saxton nfpSynergy (2008): 'A strong charity brand comes from strong beliefs and values'

motivation is not 'somebody will benefit from the money I'm sending'. I just fancy the idea of winning a new car.

Moving up the hierarchy, many donors are recruited on the promise of a '**specific action**' – 'If you give us £20, this child will go to school, this dog will be rescued, this environment saved'. Emotionally, the supporter feels moved to resolve a clear need and does the only thing within their power – they give money to the charity to provide the solution. These 'asks' are always simple, but the brief emotional engagement and immediate satisfaction they bring are both an advantage and a disadvantage. At least 50% of new supporters gained this way will not give another donation.

Many charities reinforce the engagement with incentives in a mailpack, greeting cards, name and address labels etc, then maintain the connection using more incentives. But the connection with the charity is, at best, limited.

The best early charity communications are at the third level in the hierarchy, the '**capability**' level. 'We have the capability,' they say, 'to change lives or cure problems or whatever.' There is the temptation for many charities to describe what they do rather than what they achieve when they do it, and to talk about themselves all the time. Many charities fall into that trap. But this level of motivation is higher in the hierarchy because charities are using their stature or their specialist way of working, not only to show the impact of a donation (as in the 'specific action'), but also to build a belief in the brand in the supporter's mind.

So, in an emergency, an overseas charity may ask for money for the disaster, and that money is destined for immediate relief work. But after the initial ads the charity will broaden the message. For example, the Oxfam message in Spring 2010 featured the recent Haiti disaster, but it quickly moved on to say: 'What we did successfully in Haiti we are doing in 25 other emergencies in the world, right now'. In other words: 'We have the capability to bring emergency relief to a load of different places at the same time'. For me this is cracking charity brand advertising.

On the next level up, '**values and beliefs**' become important. Good people want to stop 'bad things' because of their own beliefs and values. They use phrases like:

'This is wrong', and they want the opportunity to do something about it – hence the success of the Save the Children 'Enough is enough' ad. If a charity can operate at this level, and all the best ones do, then the supporters are buying into something that is emotionally satisfying and more long lasting. Concepts of loyalty and commitment become more appropriate. Indeed, there is no doubt that commitment to the charity increases as supporter motives rise up the hierarchy.

The pinnacle of the hierarchy is **'vision and identity'**. If a charity can express its vision clearly and emotionally and its supporters can identify their own values in similar terms, then those supporters are there for life. As a fundraiser, you might say things like: 'Together we will ensure that no child will die of preventable disease' and if that chimes with a person's own identity and they believe you, then they will support you. Unicef's 'I believe in Zero' campaign in the US was pitched at this level and has been repeated round the world. The campaign was to stop 25,000 children dying of preventable diseases **every day**. Bill Toliver, one of its authors, told me they considered alternative approaches in planning the campaign. To cut the death rate by half would be a fantastic achievement, for instance. But there was no mileage in a proposition to cut child deaths from 25,000 a day to 12,500 a day! Would perhaps, 5,000 children be an acceptable number to die every day? No, the only acceptable number is **zero**.

In Chapter 4 I described the fascinating work by Professors Sargeant and Shang, where a reference to a donor's identity increased the value of the response. Think too of the recent research into the words probate lawyers could use to ask whether their clients might leave a legacy to a charity (Chapter 10). Again, identity shows its influence. It is a supporter's sense of their own identity within their own value frame, and a vision shared with their favourite charity, that will ultimately drive their response to a request for a gift in their Will. So getting that proposition right is absolutely essential if you want to increase your legacy income.

12 It's time I stopped

If, like me, you've read the last chapter of this book first (I can never wait to finish a book to learn the end result) and if you only want to read one chapter, then it has to be the one on legacy gifts, Chapter 10. Because gifts in your supporters' Wills have the capacity to **transform** your charity's income. It may not happen within the time you work for the charity, and that is a problem for ambitious fundraisers who want quick results before they move on to other charities in their inexorable rise to the top.

Well, tough. If you really want to change your charity's fortunes, then read and implement Chapter 10. But once you've read Chapter 10, I hope you'll realise that you ought to read the rest of the book too! Because it's all about developing a new attitude that puts individual supporters and their emotions at the centre of **everything** you do as a fundraiser. Your job is to love them (to death); to make sure that, within the constraints of time, energy and reasonable investment, every one of your supporters receives great emotional experiences from your charity. That means you have to watch what they like and what produces no response. You have to reward their commitment. It's simple really: you have to treat them like you do your very good friends while remembering that they are probably a generation or two older than you.

For me, the job we do is incredibly rewarding though not without its challenges. We should stop being so polite to colleagues within the charity who forget that, without us, they'd have no salary. I am bored of the attitude of some CEOs and trustees who find our bit of fundraising, Minor Donor fundraising, really rather grubby. I had a spat at the end of 2013 with two leading members of the UK charity sector, for daring to question in an article the performance of an outgoing chief executive. This person had presided over a serious decline in fundraised and other income over the space of seven or eight years and I was questioning whether she should be receiving so much adulation.

In response to my criticisms, one senior commentator came up with the immortal lines: 'Income is not a measure of success', and: 'Income is more often to do with timing and luck'. As a fundraiser, if you didn't laugh, you'd cry!

And a chief executive of some renown made clear her views that 'delivery of vital services' is 'more important' than income. What sort of statement is that from someone who has been a CEO of a number of major UK charities? But this crass attitude exists in our sector still, and at a senior level.

Sensible people know that the delivery of services and raising the money to pay for it are equally important – you don't do one without the other. But I see fundraisers struggling against such attitudes all the time – that's why we need more fundraisers on boards and, specifically, in chief executive positions.

It's time charity trustees and chief executives remembered they have two responsibilities: spending money on the mission but, first, raising it. If they devote their attention only to the first of these, the mission will suffer and this is happening throughout the world. Fundraising would be so much more successful with the active commitment and interest of the trustees and chief executive.

Equally daft is leaving sole responsibility of the charity's brand with communication people. Many are given the power to control the message but not the responsibility for the outcome of the message, which, primarily, is donations. In the best charities of course, communications and fundraising work hand-in-glove. But, where this doesn't happen, chaos rules and donations from Minor Donors plummet. There are plenty such examples in every country I visit, and responsibility for such idiocy lies at the door of the Chief Executive, although some fundraisers are their own worst enemy: they like to keep the art of fundraising a secret, and that doesn't help anyone.

How can you get your CEO and trustees more involved? Put all your senior colleagues and trustees on your mailing lists; Tweets, campaign programmes and everything else. Make sure they see the success and failures of each through routine results summaries. Tell them how many new donors you've recruited this month or how many followers you have on Facebook. Tell them how many people have pledged a legacy and the wonderful financial implications when these are redeemed. Let them know you understand to the penny what each new donor is worth on average and how much it cost to recruit them. CEOs and trustees need to know both that fundraising is complex, creative, effective and largely complaint-free, and that it is under the close and watchful control of fundraisers who know what they are doing, long term.

And what are you doing long term? You are loving your donors (to death)!

Stephen Pidgeon

For thirty years, Stephen Pidgeon has provided fundraising services to the UK's charity sector, working with well over 200 of the nation's top charities. He founded and ran Tangible (formerly Target Direct) the leading company providing specialist fundraising services to the sector, selling it in 2007 with nearly 150 staff and a turnover to match.

Since then, he has taken his extensive fundraising experience abroad and now delivers strategic and creative support to charities in Norway, Denmark, Ireland, the US, Canada and New Zealand as well as the UK. Working with his long-term creative partner, Pauline Lockier, he still produces fundraising materials in all media for many clients, ensuring his knowledge is current.

He is in particular demand for practical workshops that deliver the charity's fundraising proposition, the absence of which is the principle cause of poor and unfocussed fundraising.

Working with Professors Adrian Sargeant and Jen Shang, Stephen now teaches direct marketing and other forms of fundraising throughout the word. He is a visiting Professor at Plymouth University and a senior member of the teaching faculty at the UK Institute of Fundraising's Academy. He teaches and delivers formal training in Ireland, Norway, New Zealand and the US.

A proficient speaker, he lectures at conferences around the world including the last four years at the AFP conference in the States. 2014 was the 25th year he has run a MasterClass in the prestigious IFC conference outside Amsterdam.

Until 2014, Stephen was an elected Trustee of the UK's Institute of Fundraising and Chairman of the Standards Committee that sets fundraising quality standards for the whole of the sector in the UK. He is now a Trustee of development agency VSO. Stephen writes a monthly column for Third Sector magazine and others in the sector press in UK and overseas. Occasionally he tweats on @stephenpidge.

Acknowledgements

I feel I should set about thanking the hundreds of fundraisers that have inspired me in my thirty years in the sector. But it would get tedious for anyone reading it and I'd be sure to miss out a name and cause unnecessary offence.

So let me confine my thanks to some close friends and colleagues who have both influenced me and put up with my definitive views for many years. First must come copywriting doyen, Pauline Lockier and sublime creative planner Nick Thomas, with both of whom I set up Target, our agency, more than twenty years ago. We built it together through exciting times when fundraising in the UK was coming of age. It was only when the agency and its sister-companies got so big that the fun started to pale!

And my good friend, stalwart fellow-teacher and ace egg-head, Adrian Sargeant, the first, and best Professor of Fundraising in the world, though now matched by the equally wonderful Jen Shang. It's because of these two that I bask in the pleasure of a Visiting Professorship at Plymouth University.

And two friends from Scandinavia. I work with Svein-Åge Johanson in Norway several times each year. I've never laughed as much as I do with him as we go from client to client. Nor worked as hard! And Copenhagen-based Malene Fregil who took my muddled script and, with consummate ease, gave it structure and direction. If you managed to finish it, it's probably because of Malene's magic.

And just one more acknowledgement. I've had a huge amount of pleasure out of the Institute of Fundraising. I chaired the Convention Committee for a few years, I was twice elected to the Board and chaired Standards Committee for six years. There is no question in my mind, every fundraiser should join the Institute; I'd make it compulsory if I could. It is so very rewarding, and if you want to get on in your career, then start contributing to its running. Volunteers are its lifeblood.

And if you are as old as me, leave it a legacy.